The Dynamics of Compliance

THE DYNAMICS OF COMPLIANCE

Supreme Court Decision-Making from a New Perspective

Richard M. Johnson

Northwestern University Press

Evanston 1967

LIBRARY OF CONGRESS CATALOG CARD NUMBER: 67–27473
Manufactured in the United States of America

Publication of this book has been aided by a grant from the State University of New York at Buffalo.

Some of the material in Chapter 9, "The Dynamics of Response," appeared in somewhat different form in an article "Compliance and Supreme Court Decision-Making" in the *Wisconsin Law Review,* Vol. 1967 (Winter), No. 1, pp. 170–85, and is used with permission of the *Wisconsin Law Review.*

Richard M. Johnson is Assistant Professor of Political Science, State University of New York at Buffalo.

To
Nancy,
Kathleen,
and Deborah

CONTENTS

ACKNOWLEDGMENTS

MANY PEOPLE have made meaningful contributions to this study and should not go unrecognized. First, the faculty and graduate students of the Department of Political Science at the University of Illinois provided me with three years of stimulating graduate study out of which this study grew. Special attention for their guidance and encouragement on this project is due Denis G. Sullivan, Jack W. Peltason, and Charles B. Hagan, of the University of Illinois. Lyman A. Kellstedt, of the State University of New York at Buffalo, and A. Don Sorensen, of Indiana University, got me interested in the kinds of problems dealt with in this book and have been important to me generally for their stimulation, criticism, and encouragement over a good number of years. David Danelski, of Yale University, John Wahlke, of the University of Iowa, and Robert H. Stern, of the State University of New York at Buffalo, read all or parts of an earlier draft of this manuscript, and their comments and criticisms are gratefully appreciated. Responsibility for the final product, of course, lies solely with the author.

I am particularly appreciative of the assistance rendered by the school superintendent of Eastville-Westville—whose name I cannot divulge—for without his cooperation and sincere interest this study could not have been consummated. Nor can I overlook the contributions of the citizens of Eastville-Westville, who tolerated, with grace, the intrusion of this outsider into their community and provided the interesting data reported in the latter portions of the book.

For providing financial assistance and time to work on this study I am indebted to the Research Foundation of the State University of New York and the Publications Committee and the Committee on the

Allocation of Funds for Faculty Research and Creative Activity of the State University of New York at Buffalo.

Finally, to my wife Nancy and our two daughters, who provided the near-perfect conditions under which graduate study was pursued and this study consummated, I dedicate this book.

RICHARD M. JOHNSON

Buffalo, New York
May, 1967

The Dynamics of Compliance

CHAPTER 1

Introduction: Decision-Making and the Supreme Court

EVENTS OF RECENT YEARS have demonstrated clearly that compliance with the rulings of the United States Supreme Court does not necessarily, universally, or automatically follow their enunciation. Though the Court told communities in 1954 and 1955 to make a start toward desegregated educational facilities,[1] a ruling which has been reaffirmed many times since by federal courts at all levels, many school boards have yet to heed this prescription. Similarly, the Court has heard a number of cases involving religious practices in public schools, some of which have been declared unconstitutional.[2] Studies of the impact of these decisions [3] as well as reports in the contemporary press indicate that these prohibited practices still take place in the classrooms of our public schools in many areas.

On the other hand, while Supreme Court decisions are limited in scope, being addressed to a particular set of circumstances at suit, it is striking that Court rulings have been implemented to a very great extent in the complete absence of specific legal obligation. Jack Greenberg, for instance, points out that most of the southern Negro children now attending integrated schools are in systems which voluntarily complied with the Court's desegregation rulings.[4] Gordon Patric also

1. *Brown v. Board of Education,* 347 U.S. 483 (1954); and 349 U.S. 294 (1955).
2. Citations and discussions of these cases will appear later.
3. Gordon M. Patric, "The Impact of a Court Decision: Aftermath of the McCollum Case," 6 *Journal of Public Law* 455 (1957); Frank J. Sorauf, *"Zorach v. Clauson:* The Impact of a Supreme Court Decision," 53 *American Political Science Review* 777 (1959); W. M. Beaney and Edward Beiser, "Prayer and Politics: The Impact of Engel and Schempp on the Political Process," 13 *Journal of Public Law* 475 (1964); Robert H. Birkby, "The Supreme Court and the Bible Belt: Tennessee Reaction to the 'Schempp' Decision," 10 *Midwest Journal of Political Science* 304 (1966).
4. *Race Relations and American Law* (New York: Columbia University Press, 1959), pp. 6–7.

reports that in the wake of the *McCollum* ruling[5] many school boards throughout the nation either discontinued or altered programs of religious education in public schools in order to bring local practices into perceived compliance with the Court's edict.[6]

It is clear, therefore, that Supreme Court determinations, particularly those involving issues of broad social concern, invoke a variety of responses. These responses in turn give substance to the policy enunciated by the Court. Consequently, to study Supreme Court decision-making and stop with an evaluation of the Court's doctrine on a particular issue or with an analysis of the voting of the justices on a number of cases, is to neglect an indispensable segment of the total judicial process. To fully comprehend this process, one must inquire into what happens, if anything, as a result of the Court's policy statement.

Supreme Court decision-making, broadly construed, is the focus of this study. Comparatively little attention will be paid to the Court itself or what it has said, as we shall be primarily concerned with outlining certain significant factors involved in the response to Court policy by individuals who are under varying degrees of obligation to act. Decision-making, therefore, is being used in the sense suggested by Lasswell and Kaplan:

> . . . a decision is an *effective* determination of policy . . . [involving] the total process of bringing about a specified course of action . . . ; the decision-making process includes application as well as formulation and promulgation of policy, [consequently] those whose acts are affected also participate in decision-making: by conformity to or disregard of the policy they help determine whether it is or is not in fact a decision. Laws are not made by legislatures alone, but by the law-abiding as well: a statute ceases to embody a law . . . in the degree that it is widely disregarded.[7]

This usage alerts us to the fact that the judicial process involves a wide range of activity. For a judicial policy to have general effect in the political system, the behavior of many individuals must be affected.

Supreme Court decision-making, therefore, will be viewed from a particular perspective. This is the perspective of compliance. Of primary concern are the elements of implementation at the local level.

5. *Illinois ex rel. McCollum v. Board of Education,* 333 U.S. 203 (1948).
6. Patric, *op. cit.*
7. Harold D. Lasswell and Abraham Kaplan, *Power and Society: A Framework for Political Inquiry* (New Haven: Yale University Press, 1950), pp. 74–75.

The Supreme Court itself, its policies, and the means by which these policies are transmitted are important in our immediate endeavor, to be sure. But these are viewed in this study from the perspective of how they impinge upon those who must effectuate policy at the level of implementation.

Although the Supreme Court decisional process will be outlined in very general terms, our attention will focus on the Court's policies concerning religious practices in public schools. The dynamics of the process may vary somewhat from issue to issue, but our treatment provides a general framework by which the process may be analyzed regardless of issue. The religion-in-public-schools issue allows us to observe the Supreme Court decisional process at one of its broadest points, as there is a great diversity of actors playing a part in the process. Decision-making here involves far more than the behavior of lawyers and judges. Whether or not there is an effective determination of policy in this area depends upon the activity of school administrators, board members, teachers, and others.

• *The Supreme Court and Eastville-Westville*

The Court has been concerned with many explosive social issues during the past two decades, but the decisions which perhaps have touched many Americans most intimately are those which have had to do with the place of religion in society. The Court on a number of well-publicized occasions has been forced to examine religious involvement in public education and to decide what the First Amendment's vague "establishment" clause would allow.[8] The course which the Court has generally followed in this regard has brought serious misgivings to many individuals of deep religious conviction. Prominent church leaders who may have little theologically in common—from Episcopal Bishop James Pike to Cardinal Cushing to evangelist Billy Graham—have spoken out against this line of decisions. Congressmen, senators, and state officials have attempted official action to offset this policy. Communities and local school boards have expressed their antagonism in a variety of ways, and Americans from all walks of life have been forced to think more abstractly about the nexus between

8. *Everson v. Board of Education,* 330 U.S. 1 (1947); *Illinois ex rel. McCollum v. Board of Education* 333 U.S. 203 (1948); *Zorach v. Clauson,* 343 U.S. 306 (1952); *Engel v. Vitale,* 370 U.S. 421 (1962); *Abington Township School District v. Schempp,* 374 U.S. 203 (1963).

their government and that which is very close to them: their relationship to the Almighty.

Religious observances or exercises in one form or another have been quite common in the public schools of America.[9] Whether or not such practices are prohibited according to the Court's general test will be decided most often by individuals closer to the scene of action, generally by local school officials or perhaps even teachers. In such instances, these officials become agents in the judicial process as they apply their conception of judicial policy to local circumstances. Seldom are courts and judges called upon to decide upon the propriety of such practices; judicial decision of this kind is likely to take place only in religiously heterogeneous communities where dissident minorities may seek court action to end the religious practices which they find so repugnant. In religiously homogeneous communities, religious practices have often continued in public school classrooms despite the Court's policies. *Inaction* on the part of the school official, as well as deliberate disregard of the Court's policy, has consequences for the judicial process in its broader aspects.

On the other hand, the fact that a community is more or less united in the belief that there should be some amount of religious worship or observances in the classrooms does not preclude the possibility that a school official will recognize a paramount responsibility to bring classroom practices under his jurisdiction into perceived congruence with the policy enunciated by the Court. And, if he does so, it does not necessarily follow that there will be a period of strife in the community or that the school official's job will be put in jeopardy. Even in religiously homogeneous communities which project their intense religiosity into their school curricula, action by school officials under the aegis of Court policy may strike a responsive chord in the community or at least in a significant segment of it.

Our study involves just this situation. It is concerned with the implementation of Supreme Court policy in a rural school district in central Illinois. The school district is composed of two small villages—pseudonymously labeled Eastville and Westville—and the surrounding fertile farmlands. A brand-new school superintendent came into this very homogeneous Fundamentalist-Protestant community and halted the traditional prayer before lunch in the school cafeterias. The superintendent considered this practice repugnant per-

9. See, for example, Richard B. Dierenfield, *Religion in American Public Schools* (Washington, D.C.: Public Affairs Press, 1962).

sonally and felt that it was clearly contrary to what the Supreme Court had said in the *Engel v. Vitale* [10] and *Abington School District v. Schempp* [11] decisions. To the surprise of many, including the superintendent himself, community conflict did not ensue. A fuller description of the district and an account of the events surrounding the implementation of the policy are contained in Chapter 7.

Admittedly, from the data drawn from Eastville-Westville we are not going to be able to generalize about the processes of effectuation of Supreme Court policy at the level of implementation. We are similarly unable to formulate hypotheses and rigorously test them in this field situation; the relative paucity of directly applicable theory and research prevents this. We are able, however, to test in a preliminary way the efficacy of the analytical framework which will be presented in succeeding chapters. Our work can thus be viewed as an exploratory study which may lead to the development of hypotheses and more systematic testing at a later time.

In Chapter 2 we shall present the major theoretical argument relating to the bases on which Supreme Court decisions are accepted, rejected, or modified in some sense. In Chapters 3, 4, 5, and 6 the Court as the originator of the policies, the nature of the policy statements themselves, and the channels through which the policy statements are transmitted will be considered from the perspective of their contributions to the implementation of policy. Finally, the response of the Eastville-Westville community to Supreme Court policy will be reported in Chapters 7, 8, and 9.

Robert Michels has contended that it is

> futile to discuss the *raison d'être* of authority. Authority exists and will continue to exist as it has always existed in one form or another, because it has its basis in traits deeply rooted in the human mind and because it answers the practical needs of society.[12]

While we basically agree with Michels concerning the roots of authority, this study is precisely an attempt to deal with the *raison d'être* of the authority of the United States Supreme Court as well as other underlying bases of the Court's influence.

10. 370 U.S. 421 (1962).
11. 374 U.S. 203 (1963).
12. "Authority," *Encyclopedia of the Social Sciences* (New York: Macmillan, 1930), Vol. II, p. 320.

CHAPTER 2

Bases of Acceptance or Rejection of Supreme Court Policy

By accepting Lasswell and Kaplan's notion that "a decision is an *effective* determination of policy . . . the total process of bringing about a specified course of action,"[1] we are conceptualizing decision-making in a relational sense. Activity is entailed, not only on the part of those attempting to affect the behavior of others but on the part of those whose acts are to be affected. As for Supreme Court decision-making, it is compliant behavior on the part of others that gives substance to the Court's determinations. If the Court announces a policy and no compliant behavior ensues, then there is no decision.

The emphasis in this study, as we have said, will be on the compliance side of this dyadic relationship. Students of the Supreme Court have paid little attention to compliance; concerned primarily with what the justices have said, they have concentrated on the actual words used in decisions or have compiled accumulations of the votes cast by individual justices over a period of time.[2] But this gives an incomplete view of the decision-making process. It is the purpose of our study to

1. H. D. Lasswell and A. Kaplan, *Power and Society: A Framework for Political Inquiry* (New Haven: Yale University Press, 1950).

2. This shortcoming has been noted in recent years by the following: Glendon Schubert, "Behavioral Research in Public Law," 57 *American Political Science Review* 433 (1963); Samuel Krislov, "The Perimeters of Power: Patterns of Compliance and Opposition to Supreme Court Decisions," paper delivered at the Annual Meeting of the American Political Science Association, New York City, Sept. 4–7, 1963; Arthur S. Miller, "On the Need for 'Impact Analysis' of Supreme Court Decisions," 53 *Georgetown Law Journal* 365 (1965). Notable exceptions to this are the efforts noted in Chapter 1, note 3, *supra,* and that of Jack W. Peltason, *Fifty-Eight Lonely Men* (New York: Harcourt, Brace & World, 1961).

fill out the picture by describing the Supreme Court decision-making system from the compliance perspective.

• *Supreme Court Power*

Even in cases involving perhaps the most severely divisive issues in our society—racial integration and the church-state question—widespread compliance with the Court's determinations may be observed. Why does this conformity to the Court's expectations follow? The answer, it is suggested, lies partially in the nature of the power relationships existing between the Court and those affected by its rulings.[3]

Power is defined here as merely the ability of *O* to influence *P*.[4] This ability does not derive necessarily from attributes possessed by *O* singly. The successful execution of influence depends upon the ability of *O* to move *P* in the desired direction by tapping certain motive bases, fulfilling certain needs, or affecting certain values of *P*.[5] Power is often viewed in a rather narrow fashion, suggesting that it is based solely on the availability of severe sanctions by *O* to obtain *P*'s compliance.[6] While this is an important basis for a power relationship, it is merely one of a number of bases. These various bases are discussed below, and their particular relevance to Supreme Court decision-making is indicated.[7]

»*Coercive Power*

The coercive power of *O* over *P* is based on *P*'s expectation that *O* will invoke severe sanctions if behavior compliant with an order is not

3. Initially we shall speak in terms of a simple compliance-noncompliance dichotomy, with the understanding that this is a gross but convenient oversimplification. Later we shall address ourselves to the problem of refining the concept.

4. In the general explication of the power relationship, *O* refers to a social agent which may be an individual, group, or any social entity such as the Supreme Court. *P*, of course, refers to the object of the influence attempt.

5. As with most current conceptualizations, power here is viewed in a relational sense. The literature on power is extensive in the social sciences, but see, for example: Robert A. Dahl, "The Concept of Power," 2 *Behavioral Science* 201 (1957); William Riker, "Some Ambiguities in the Notion of Power," 58 *American Political Science Review* 341 (1964); and Dorwin Cartwright (ed.), *Studies in Social Power* (Ann Arbor: University of Michigan Press, 1959).

6. See for example, Lasswell and Kaplan, *op. cit.*, as well as Peter Bachrach and Morton S. Baratz, "Decisions and Nondecisions: An Analytical Framework," 57 *American Political Science Review* 632 (1963).

7. This argument primarily derives from John R. P. French, Jr., and Bertram M. Raven, "The Bases of Social Power," Chap. 9 in Cartwright (ed.), *op. cit.*

forthcoming. *P* clearly knows what is expected of him and recognizes that *O* has the wherewithal and the serious intent to impose such sanctions if compliant behavior does not ensue.

Coercive power has limited relevance to Supreme Court decision-making. The Court uses it to achieve compliance with its policies in those instances where it has been called upon to resolve a specific controversy. In such instances the Supreme Court hears a case, announces its determination, and directs that certain behavior take place or cease on the part of the principals involved. The legal mechanism—the lower courts and their staffs—are thus called upon to provide an important aspect of "observability" or surveillance to ascertain whether or not the decision is complied with.[8] Other devices which the Court may utilize to achieve compliant behavior are injunctions, writs of mandamus, and contempt-of-court citations.

Coercive power can also be operative where the Court has not become directly involved in a local situation. If a Court order strikes down practices which are analogous to those going on in another, unrelated, community, the "precedent" can become a powerful tool in the hands of individuals who recognize that they can use the ruling as a wedge to have their claims processed. Compliance on the part of relevant public officials may result because of fear that noncompliance may ultimately bring punishment via the coercive powers of government. Recent civil rights legislation, it is to be noted, increases the observability potential—hence the coercive power—of the federal judiciary by permitting the U.S. Attorney General to initiate suits in the federal courts involving school desegregation and voter registration under specified conditions.

Compliant behavior may also result from social pressure. General acceptance of legal norms and the role of the Supreme Court in the political system cause noncompliant behavior to be considered unacceptable. When a norm is enunciated, whether by Court or legislature, the usual reaction involves compliance.[9] In a given situation, broad segments of the population would punish noncomplying "deviants" through various techniques of social ostracism. Here model societal behavior is that which threatens the noncompliant.

8. For a study of the importance of observability in relation to coercive power see B. Raven and J. R. P. French, "Legitimate Power, Coercive Power and Observability in Social Influence," 21 *Sociometry* 83 (1958).

9. This could be behind the general repugnance toward many of the techniques employed by civil rights demonstrators, even of a nonviolent nature.

This form of power relationship may be observed in the context of more intimate social groups as well. If a group with which one identifies is supportive of a Supreme Court policy, the individual, in order to maintain a satisfying relationship with the group, must adhere to the position that the group takes on the issue. The Presbyterian, for instance, may support the Court's school-prayer decisions even though he may have little direct interest in the matter or sympathy for the policy announced by the Court. He does so because he knows or perceives that his church is supportive of the Court in this regard, and his acceptance of the position allows him to maintain his satisfying identification with the church.[10]

In these instances compliance on the part of *P* results from a threat of deprivation of his particular need for broad social or narrow group approval. The resources which may be utilized for such deprivation, however, reside in social relationships and only circuitously can be attributed to the resources of the Court itself. Since compliant behavior nevertheless results from the threat of such sanctions, they are potentially an important source for compliance with Supreme Court policy.

»*Legitimate Power*

Perhaps the most pervasive basis for Supreme Court influence in the broadest sense is that associated with the notion of legitimacy. Legitimate power derives from the *conviction* on the part of *P* that *O* has a moral right to influence the behavior of *P* and that *P* has an obligation to accept this influence. David Easton has succinctly stated the nature of this relationship when he writes that a sense of legitimacy stems

> from the conviction on the part of the member that it is right and proper for him to accept and obey the authorities and to abide by the requirements of the regime. It reflects the fact that in some vague or explicit way he sees these objects as conforming to his own moral principles, his own sense of what is right and proper in the political sphere.
>
> The strength of support implicit in this attitude derives from the fact that it is not contingent on specific inducements or rewards of any kind, except in the very long run. On a day-to-day basis, if there is a strong inner conviction of the moral validity of the authorities or regime,

10. Empirical support for this aspect of coercive power is found in Herbert C. Kelman, "Compliance, Identification and Internalization: Three Processes of Attitude Change," 2 *Journal of Conflict Resolution* 51 (1958).

> support may persist even in the face of repeated deprivations attributed to the outputs of the authorities or their failure to act.[11]

The great difference between this form of power and coercive power resides in the fact that compliant behavior ensues here without either the perception or threat of available sanctions.

As with coercive power, legitimate power may take a number of forms in relation to the Supreme Court decision-making situation. One such form, which Max Weber labeled "legality," is influence based on rationally created rules, such as constitutions, statutes, or decrees.[12] Those who act in accordance with these are viewed as persons who may legitimately affect the behavior of others.

Acceptance of the Constitution as the basic political formula involves a concomitant acceptance of the Supreme Court as an integral component of the political mechanism established therein. Thus individuals perceive compliance with Court-made policy as one of a number of necessary obligations required by their commitment to the general political system. Legitimacy, in this sense, is enmeshed in the network of norms and roles of the political system.

Weber also points toward a second form of legitimate power when he speaks of "traditional domination." Here influence rests on factors which presumably have always existed, such as patriarchalism, where there is rule by the father or husband. This notion of legitimacy seems congruent with that advanced by Seymour Lipset. To him, "Legitimacy involves the capacity of the system to engender and maintain the belief that the existing political institutions are the most appropriate ones for the society." [13] In the patriarchal society the belief was perpetuated that it was appropriate for the father as head of the clan to make certain policies binding on the rest. Tradition similarly stands behind a recognition of the courts as appropriate institutions for handling certain forms of controversy. The judicial process has been set apart from other elements of the political system in a variety of ways, and the manner in which disputes brought before it are resolved is quite different from that characteristic of the other branches. There is a general consensus that certain matters should be handled by the judi-

11. *A Systems Analysis of Political Life* (New York: John Wiley & Sons, 1965), p. 278.

12. H. H. Gerth and C. Wright Mills (editors and translators) *From Max Weber: Essays in Sociology* (New York: Oxford University Press, 1958), pp. 295–97.

13. *Political Man* (Garden City: Doubleday & Co., Inc., 1960), p. 77.

ciary while others come more appropriately within the purview of the so-called "political" branches. The Court has explicitly recognized this in its enunciation from time to time of the "political question" doctrine.[14] In general, however, the Supreme Court has been viewed as the ultimate and appropriate interpreter of the Constitution; this function, not derivative from the Constitution but announced by the Court itself,[15] has been reinforced by traditional acceptance.

A final relevant form of legitimacy has to do, not with the source of the order, as do the first two forms we have discussed, but rather with its content. For example, the Court's interpretation of the "establishment of religion" clause may be accepted by individuals because it is in accord with their idea of what the relationship *should be* between the church and state—the source of the message being, in the main, irrelevant. This form of legitimate power corresponds to that labeled by Kelman as "internalization." Internalization occurs

> when an individual accepts influence because the content of the induced behavior—the ideas and actions of which it is composed—is intrinsically rewarding. He adopts the induced behavior because it is congruent with his value system. He may consider it useful for the solution of a problem or find it congenial to his needs. Behavior adopted in this fashion tends to be integrated with the individual's existing values.[16]

Supreme Court decisions, as we shall see in Chapter 4, are not merely brief announcements of the results of the Court's deliberations to the principals involved in the immediate suit. Rather, these orders are usually definitive, presenting a rationale for the policy in the immediate case and demonstrating the benefits to be realized from general observance of it. The orders are obviously not only addressed to the principals but present persuasive argumentation designed to influence a broad audience. The opinions have what Friedrich labels "authority," which is to him "a quality of communication" which has "the potentiality of reasoned elaboration." [17] What the Court may say in the substance of its opinion may be viewed as "right" or expressive

14. See, for example, *Luther v. Borden,* 7 Howard 1 (1849), and *Colegrove v. Green* 328 U.S. 549 (1946).

15. *Marbury v. Madison,* 1 Cranch 137 (1803).

16. Kelman, *op. cit.,* p. 53.

17. C. J. Friedrich, "Authority, Reason and Discretion," in Friedrich (ed.), *Authority* (Cambridge: Harvard University Press, 1958), pp. 35–36, quoted and discussed in Bachrach and Baratz, *op. cit.,* pp. 638–639.

of the highest of values; hence one has the obligation to conform to the Court's expectations.

»Expert Power

This type of power is based on a perception by *P* that *O* has some particular knowledge or expertise in a given area. *P* has a "need for understanding" or a need for determining "social reality" and perceives that *O* has informational or knowledge resources by which such needs may be satiated. Consequently, *O*'s influence is accepted. Taking a pill at the insistence of a doctor, buying stocks on the advice of a broker, and accepting a lawyer's counsel in legal affairs are instances of perception of expert power.

This, too, can conceivably be a basis upon which some accept Supreme Court influence. Problems of constitutional interpretation and statutory construction are beyond the experience of most Americans, even though such problems may have great and intimate relevance to their lives. What are the dimensions of the concept of "separation of church and state"? Does this bar the traditional Christmas assembly in the public schools? Does "freedom of speech" protect the utterances of known Communists? Does the "equal protection of the law" clause demand that both houses of state legislatures be established on the basis of population? Such questions are of deep concern to many, and some may perceive that the justices have the competence objectively to determine what the Constitution "really" says in regard to them. To be sure, such questions are emotionally charged, and evaluations of the Court's handling of them often depends on the congruence of the decisions and individual value systems. On a wide range of issues, particularly those not as emotionally laden as the above examples, expertise may be a quite pervasive basis for compliance because of the esoteric nature of legal questions, the technical language in which they are discussed, and the manner in which legal matters are dealt with.

From this discussion of the underlying bases of Court power, it is obvious that they are not mutually exclusive but mutually reinforcing. That is to say, the Constitution, as the basic statement of the network of norms and roles in the political system, not only provides for the Court itself but also provides that it be the appropriate body for handling certain forms of conflict. Article III of the Constitution, for example, specifically delineates those instances in which the Court has original jurisdiction while stating that in all other cases it has appellate jurisdiction. On this constitutional basis, statutory enactments have further elaborated the appropriate scope of Supreme Court activity and the proper channels of access to the Court.

Furthermore, the Court—by tradition an elite, expert group—has been set apart from other branches of government and the citizenry in a variety of ways, to be discussed in Chapter 3. The justices have been removed from the exigencies of political life. Consequently, the results of their deliberations, the content of the orders themselves, may be perceived to be basically "right" and "proper" and not the product of partisan political necessity.

Finally, a coordinate branch of government—the executive—has the constitutional responsibility for seeing to it that the laws are faithfully executed. Under this broad grant, supplemented by subsequent legislative enactments, the executive branch can observe the extent to which behavior compliant with Court rulings obtains and can, if necessary, implement rulings through forceful action. Rather than being a set of discrete elements then, these bases of Court power are actually interrelated components of a system of compliance.

A summary of the argument thus far is in order. A decision is being viewed in its broadest sense. That is, it involves not only the enunciation of a policy on the part of the Supreme Court, but compliant behavior on the part of others is also entailed. This compliance may ensue as a result of a system of power relationships existing between the Court and those who are affected by its policies. Components of this compliance system have been referred to as coercive power, legitimate power, and expert power, with legitimate power being viewed as the most pervasive ingredient in the decisional structure under consideration.

The Court may attempt to induce compliant behavior through the use of techniques characteristic of the various power bases discussed. That is, with respect to legitimate power, it may attempt to incorporate in the text of a decision persuasive argumentation designed to bring about the desired response by those who are not directly involved in the suit. By the same token, compliance may ensue because of more than one of the underlying power bases. Individuals who agree with the logic of the Court's argument and also acknowledge that it is the Court's responsibility to make such determinations may comply on these or other bases. Hence, the Supreme Court decisional system may be meaningfully analyzed not only from the perspective of the Court, which is attempting to stimulate broad compliance with its orders, but from the perspective of those who are under varying obligations to act.

• *Compliance and Cognitive Consistency*

The forces impinging on individuals at the level of implementation do not originate solely with the Court, and often there are counterpressures against the Court's policy. The policy enunciated by the Court touches individuals who are participants in ongoing social processes which the Court is attempting to alter. The coercive, legitimate, and expert bases of Supreme Court power are important factors supporting the Court's position, but there are also compelling reasons for the particular social processes involved. It is important to consider the context within which actors at the level of implementation function. For instance, the people of a religiously oriented community may feel that a daily recognition of a Supreme Being in the public school can be an important factor in the spiritual and moral development of their youth, a development at least as important as that involving intellectual skills. For many, then, the Court's argument that such a practice is an unconstitutional "establishment of religion" pales when it is applied to matters which involve questions of ultimate reality. Only when we appreciate more fully the totality of the forces impinging on individuals at the level of implementation can we account for the varying responses made to Supreme Court policy and thus see this decisional structure in greater perspective.

As noted before, the coercive-power base of the Supreme Court is largely limited to those instances where the Court has specifically ruled on a set of circumstances. However, general compliance with rulings of the Court cannot depend upon this measure of legal observation and must necessarily involve other sorts of pressures. It is hypothesized that pressures of a very special kind are brought to bear upon a wide range of actors motivating them to alter activity to make it consistent with rulings of the United States Supreme Court. Who these actors are, of course, depends upon the issue involved and the unique characteristics of the decision-making structure in the particular community. Since we are primarily concerned with the Court's religion-in-public-schools policy, implementation is centered around school-board members and school administrators. The processes of compliance and noncompliance may be studied by analysis of the kinds of pressures impinging upon the actors who have to implement the policy and those who are somewhat affected by it.

The pressures to which we refer are those which are explained by the various theories of "cognitive consistency." Subsumed under the label of consistency are the concepts of "cognitive balance," "congruity," and "cognitive dissonance." [18] Basic to this type of theory is the notion that "the human organism tries to establish internal harmony, consistency, or congruity among his opinions, attitudes, knowledge and values. That is, there is a drive toward consonance among his cognitions." [19] Of most immediate relevance for our purposes is the notion of cognitive balance. This theory assumes that when there is an imbalanced cognitive state, tensions are produced and forces are generated to restore the natural balance. Knowledge of Supreme Court policies—specifically those which have broad social import, such as the recent ones banning prescribed prayers in public school classrooms—may or may not upset the internal "balance" of relevant actors. There will be no imbalance if the ongoing social process involved is consistent with the policy enunciated by the Court. For example, if the Court bans official classroom devotions but such practices are not a part of the school's activities, the practices and the policy are already congruent, and knowledge of both leaves the balance of the organism undisturbed.

Cognitive balance will be disturbed if the actor knows of a Court ruling which bans practices analogous to those currently taking place in his immediate social system. If a school system is accustomed to having required classroom prayers and the superintendent knows about the relevant Court rulings, an imbalance will be created and tensions will be produced. According to consistency theory, forces will then be generated to restore the normal state of balance.

One means for restoring balance is to change overt behavior and the cognitive elements associated with it. Thus, sanctioned public school prayer may be abandoned by responsible school officials to bring knowledge of existing practices into balance with knowledge of relevant Court rulings that ban such practices.

18. The most elaborately worked-out theory is that of Leon Festinger, *A Theory of Cognitive Dissonance* (Evanston: Row, Peterson & Co., 1957). Similar concepts are "cognitive balance" as developed by Fritz Heider, "Attitudes and Cognitive Organization," 21 *Journal of Psychology* 107 (1946); and "congruity" introduced by C. E. Osgood and P. H. Tannenbaum in "The Principle of Congruity in the Prediction of Attitude Change," 62 *Psychological Review* 42 (1955). Robert Zajonc recognizes their similarity and subsumes these concepts under the label of consistency theory in his "Concepts of Balance, Congruity, and Dissonance," 24 *Public Opinion Quarterly* 280 (1960).

19. Festinger, *op. cit.*, p. 260.

The altering of overt behavior will, however, be difficult in many instances. The ongoing activity may have been a manifestation of deeply rooted values in the community which many individuals would not wish to discard summarily. Consequently a difficult decision will be faced by officials if local practices are perceived to run contrary to Supreme Court policy. There will be, on one side of the question, cognitive elements corresponding to the positive characteristics of the ongoing social process. Let us consider, using the religion-in-schools issue, that the community may be very homogeneous in its religious orientation and that it has projected its deep religiosity into the curriculum of the public school system. There may be no local dissenters to this long-practiced custom. On the other hand, there likewise are cognitive elements corresponding to the positive characteristics of complying with Supreme Court rulings. There may be a recognition that the legal system rests in great measure upon voluntary compliance with the law. Certainly, it is dangerous to demonstrate to the youth of

the community a blatant disregard for the law, even though one may disagree deeply with its substance.

An official may be faced with just this sort of choice—a choice between two alternatives each having both positive and negative characteristics. Nevertheless, a decision has to be made, and the making of the choice may not restore cognitive balance to the decision-maker. A choice of one of the alternatives obviously means not choosing the other and the positive aspects associated with it. Once the decision has been made—when the decision-maker commits himself to one course of action over the other—a new type of imbalance is generated along with pressures to restore the balance. It is at this point that *cognitive-dissonance* theory—a special type of consistency theory—gains specific relevance.[20] Cognitive-dissonance theory essentially accounts for postdecisional phenomena contrasted to balance theory, which may be used to account for the dynamics of the predecisional phase, as illustrated above. After an actor commits himself to an action and discards its alternative, a "postdecisional dissonance" is produced. Here "the cognitive elements corresponding to the positive characteristics of the rejected alternative, and those corresponding to the negative characteristics of the chosen alternative are dissonant with the action that has

20. As we move to the postdecisional phase, the cognitive-dissonance theory of Festinger is appropriate. For a discussion of the importance of "commitment" for dissonance theory see Jack W. Brehm and Arthur R. Cohen, *Explorations in Cognitive Dissonance* (New York: John Wiley & Sons, Inc., 1962).

been taken."[21] The pressure of such dissonance, then, activates pressures to reduce the dissonance and to bring consonance among cognitions.

Going back to matters of substantive concern for examples, assume that a school superintendent made the decision to abandon religious practices in the schools of his system as a result of Supreme Court policy. While discontinuing the school prayers makes the practices congruent with the Court's policy, the cognitive elements surrounding the new behavior are dissonant with those involved in the rejected alternative, e.g., the positive benefits to the pupil inherent in daily devotions in schools.

According to this theory, there will be pressure toward consonance among cognitions. That is to say, the dissonance may be reduced in a number of ways which have the effect of increasing the desirability of the chosen alternative and/or decreasing the desirability of the rejected alternative. A number of modes of dissonance reduction will be suggested below, along with their implications for the Supreme Court decision-making situation.

One such mechanism is that of *bolstering*—"relating one or the other of the two cognitive objects in a balanced way to other valued objects, thereby minimizing the relative imbalance in the structure."[22] In other words, dissonance can be drowned out by adding positive elements to the chosen alternative. For example, cognitions about the Supreme Court ruling can be bolstered through acknowledgment of the power bases noted above. The legitimacy of the Court to make such pronouncements, the cogency of its arguments, or its expert capacities may be recognized in order to bolster compliance with the policy.

Similarly, the affected individual may bolster his chosen action by drawing upon factors from the social system within which he operates. He may perceive his role as involving, in part, compliance with Supreme Court determinations. Also, he may perceive that others expect him to behave in ways directed by the Court. For instance, the school administrator may personally feel or perceive that members of his clientele group—the school-district parents—or others higher or lower in the bureaucratic structure may expect actions carried out in compliance with directives of the Supreme Court. In addition to these factors associated with a specific role, other reference groups may perform this

21. Festinger, *op. cit.*, p. 261.
22. Robert P. Abelson, "Modes of Resolution of Belief Dilemmas," 3 *The Journal of Conflict Resolution* 343 (December, 1959).

same sort of function. School administrators, for example, may look to a variety of reference groups supportive of the decision to provide a normative standard by which the Court's ruling may be evaluated.

Denial is another mechanism which may be utilized in such circumstances, alone or in combination with bolstering. Denial is "a direct attack upon one or both of the cognitive elements or the relation between them." [23] In a case involving a behavior change in the direction of congruence with the Court's prayer decision, dissonance may be reduced by an attack on the rejected alternative behavior, that is, required prayers in the public school classroom. For instance, the efficacy of such arrangements to enhance either moral or spiritual development may be *denied.*

Transcendence is suggested as a third method of dissonance reduction. In transcendence, "elements are built up and combined into large units organized on a superordinate level." [24] This transcendent structure is then consonant with the other cognitive element. For example, when the Supreme Court decides that officially prescribed prayer in public schools is unconstitutional, positive cognitions of these ongoing exercises in such schools and cognition of the decision are directly related in a dissonant situation:

(+) ———————————————— (−)
A. Religion B. Prayer decision

A transcendent structure, "separation of church and state," may be invoked to reduce the dissonance caused by discontinuing the practices in pursuance of the decision:

Religion (+) ———————————————— (−)
State (+) B. Prayer decision

A. Separation of church and state

Here, positive cognitions associated with religion are retained but are combined with positive cognitions associated with the state. However, the relationship, as indicated by the broken line, is a dissociated one.
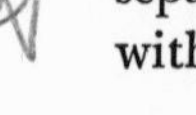
That is, there is a recognition that religion and the state are to be kept separate for the health of each, and this idea is now directly associated with a negative Court ruling concerning school prayers.

23. *Ibid.*, p. 344.
24. *Ibid.*, p. 349.

Of particular importance to the Supreme Court decisional situation is a mode of resolution referred to as *differentiation,* the "splitting of a cognitive element into two parts with a strong dissociative relation between the parts." [25] One portion of the split element may then be associatively related to the other cognitive element, while the other portion will be dissociatively related; the structure thus comes into balance. For example, when the Court decides that prayer in the public school is unconstitutional, positive cognitions of ongoing practices and negative cognitions of the decisions are directly related in a dissonant situation:

⊕ ———————————————— ⊖
A. Practices B. Decisions

Either by altering the behavior to a certain degree or by altering one's cognitions about the ongoing practices, it may be possible to *differentiate* the program from "previous" practices and view it as being consonant with the decision of the Court:

A. Acceptable practices ⊕ - - - - - - - - - - ⊖ B. Decision
A′. Unacceptable practices ⊖ ———————— ⊖

Thus state-prescribed prayers, required Bible reading, etc., may be unconstitutional (A′); however, the essence of the program may be retained by "allowing" teachers to continue such practices in the classroom as a matter of individual teacher discretion (A), a matter which was not covered by the Court's policy statement. A good example of this occurred after the *McCollum* ruling against religious education in public school classrooms. "Released-time" programs, whereby students were excused from classes to attend religious instruction in outside religious facilities, were cognitively differentiated from those practices declared unconstitutional, while the essence of the program remained in tact. Later the Supreme Court in fact sanctioned such differentiation! [26]

Our discussion has dealt with instances where effort is made psychologically to bring cognitions of ongoing social processes into

25. *Ibid.,* p. 345.
26. *Zorach v. Clauson,* 343 U.S. 306 (1952).

congruence with Supreme Court determination. In this sense, particularly in the cases where overt behavior has changed, the psychological pressure resulting from cognitive imbalance and dissonance may be viewed as a catalyst in the compliance process. By the same token, however, behavior which may be totally incongruent with a Supreme Court order may be perpetuated and cognitions may be brought into balance through the same modes of resolution noted above. That is, the imbalance or dissonance produced by bringing cognitions concerning a Supreme Court decision into contact with cognitions concerning opposing overt behavior can be reduced in other ways than by changing behavior. One means may be through the fabrication of a transcendent structure. Once again an unbalanced situation exists due to cognitions of ongoing religious exercises in the public schools and cognitions of a Supreme Court decision striking such practices down as unconstitutional:

(+)————————————(−)

A. Religious exercises   B. Supreme Court decision

To some, however, the decision may be sadly viewed as just one more step in the growing secularization of American society with its attendant evils:

A. Religious exercises (+) - - - - - - - -
(−) Supreme Court decision
(−) Divorce rate
(−) Crime
(−) Corruption
(−) Juvenile delinquency
B. Secularization of American society

The religious exercises having positive affect are thus dissociated from this threatening transcendent structure, and there is no pressure to alter existing behavior.

Other modes of resolution may be cited as potentially supportive of behavior contrary to what the Court has deemed constitutionally feasible. Denial, for instance, may be invoked to attack directly the cognitive elements related to the decision. The Court may be viewed as exceeding its legitimate range of power. To be sure, the Court has a job to do, but it has gone too far when it tells us whether or not our schoolchildren can pray in school. Or the Court's expertise may be acknowledged in some areas while the problem of the proper relationship between church and state may be viewed as beyond the competence of the jurist. The judges themselves may be attacked as atheistic, pro-Communistic secularists.

By the same token, cognitive elements related to a particular program may be bolstered by the addition of a number of elements supportive of the program. A number of compelling moral arguments for the retention of religious exercises in the public schools can be easily imagined. The benefit to the child of a "little prayer" before school certainly offsets knowing that one is not doing exactly what the Supreme Court has said.

In summary, if a decision is received by those who are affected by it at the level of implementation, the cognitive elements related to the ruling will be either consistent or inconsistent with cognitions concerning relevant ongoing social processes in the community. If these elements cannot be considered consistent with each other—that is, if one element implies the obverse of the other—a psychological imbalance is created and pressures or tensions arise to return the organism to a balanced state. Such balance may be restored by changing overt behavior to bring it into perceived compliance with the Court's policy. Hence, balance theory provides an important explanation for certain aspects of voluntary compliance in the Supreme Court decision-making situation.

A change in overt behavior, however, is not always the mode of resolution adopted for problems of cognitive imbalance, nor does it necessarily restore balance. A decision is made to adopt one alternative and reject another which, in many cases, creates dissonance and the accompanying pressure toward consonance in cognitions. This dissonance can be reduced in a number of ways at the cognitive level, as illustrated above, by increasing the attractiveness of the chosen alternative and decreasing that of the rejected alternative. These same processes may similarly be utilized to justify behavior either congruent with or contrary to Supreme Court policy.

Supreme Court rulings, this suggests, may invoke a range of responses. To use the term "compliance" to characterize this process is rather unfortunate, for this seems to suggest a single approved response to a Court ruling. In certain instances, to be sure, such a view would be entirely satisfactory. When the Court rules that the religious-education program be halted in the public schools of Champaign, Illinois, there is only a single proper response by those who are directly responsible for the program. If a county clerk is mandamused to carry out his election-registration responsibilities, once again a narrow-gauge notion of compliance is adequate. In such instances, the compliance-noncompliance dichotomy will not lead to difficulty.

A much more complex set of problems is involved when we deal with instances which have not *directly* been the subject of litigation. The Court has stated that a school board may not prescribe that the Lord's Prayer be said or that the Bible be read in devotional services in public schools. Does compliance with this mean that a teacher may not lead her students in a prayer before lunch in the cafeteria of the school? Does this mean that the Bible may not be read and used in public schools as history or as an example of a certain literary form? Krislov is on point when he notes that ". . . what is or is not compliance belongs in the realm not of 'objective reality' but rather is defined by what is acceptable . . . ; the zone of compliance will vary based upon social perception." [27]

An analytical scheme has thus been presented to account for variations in response to Supreme Court policy. The utility of this scheme will be judged later, when we observe the dynamics of response to the Court's religion-in-schools policy in the Eastville-Westville setting. Before focusing upon this community, we must consider other components of the judicial process from the perspective of the scheme presented in this chapter. Consequently, we shall now view, in four successive chapters, the Supreme Court as the source of public policy, the nature of the policy statements made by the Court with respect to religion in the schools, and finally the various channels utilized to transmit Supreme Court policy. Again it is to be emphasized that these components will be viewed primarily in terms of their contributions to compliance.

27. Krislov, *op. cit.,* p. 11.

CHAPTER 3

The Supreme Court as Message Source

THE UNITED STATES Supreme Court has been characterized as the "least dangerous branch" of government.[1] In terms of the coercive power described in Chapter 2, this is indeed a fair characterization. It has been remarked on numerous occasions that the Court possesses neither the sword nor the purse to ensure compliance with its orders. This point is driven home by Andrew Jackson's legendary retort to Marshall's holding in the *Cherokee Indian Case:*[2] "John Marshall has made his decision, now let him enforce it."

Certainly there are no troops at the direct disposal of the Court. If troops are needed, they must come from a concurring executive branch. The Court itself must necessarily operate within a rather rigid and narrow framework, having few alternative lines of action for dealing with the noncompliant.[3] It may hear only those cases brought to it, and it can only reasonably rely upon action supportive of its rulings from the inferior courts of the system, which, in turn, have a relatively meager arsenal of weapons at their command. The lower courts may ensure that the rulings of the high Court are implemented in those instances directly at suit, but they are otherwise limited only to the cases subsequently presented to them for litigation.

This is not to say that compliance results only from the bayonet and

1. Alexander Hamilton in *Federalist* 78. This is discussed more recently in Alexander M. Bickel, *The Least Dangerous Branch: The Supreme Court at the Bar of Politics* (Indianapolis: Bobbs-Merrill Co., Inc., 1962).

2. *The Cherokee Indian Nation v. Georgia,* 5 Peters 1 (1831).

3. It has been suggested that a measure of power of an actor is the number of open lines of action available to him. E. Abramson, H. A. Cutler, R. W. Kautz, and M. Mendelson, "Social Power and Commitment: A Theoretical Statement," 23 *American Sociological Review* 15 (1958).

physical coercion. The fact is that in certain matters of broadest social significance dealt with by the Court—such as religious practices in the public schools, school desegregation, and legislative redistricting—behavioral change in the direction sanctioned by the Court frequently does take place in the absence of a Court order of any kind, as we pointed out in Chapter 2.

The Court has other sources of strength. In Chapter 2 we suggested that coercive power was just one basis upon which Supreme Court influence stands. Legitimate power and the power of expertise were suggested as even more important bases of the Court's influence. Here we shall discuss more fully certain characteristics of the Court which lend themselves to the voluntary acceptance of its policy statements.

The availability of tools of coercion is not necessary, since changes in behavior as well as opinion—hence acceptance and compliance—may occur in their absence. This is due in part to the nature of the judicial process and the degree to which it is representative of communication processes in general. Opinion change results from the creation of a greater incentive for making a new implicit response than for making the accustomed one.[4] There are three major classes of stimuli present in a communication situation capable of producing shifts in incentive for making the new responses which may be anticipatory of behavior change: (1) the observable characteristics of the perceived source of the communication; (2) the setting in which individuals are exposed to the communication; and (3) the content elements of the communication itself. Conceptualizing the judicial process as a communications process helps us to understand the voluntary acceptance of and compliance with the Court's "messages."

In this chapter we shall concern ourselves with the first class of stimuli—the observable characteristics of the perceived source of the communication. Success of a communication is "significantly affected by cues as to the communicator's intentions, expertness, and trustworthiness." [5] The Supreme Court as a message source has been endowed with a certain aura and carries on its work in a particular manner which is capable of producing incentives for acceptance of its messages. However, attitudes toward the communicator are but one factor in the communication situation, and they interact with other factors impor-

4. Carl I. Hovland, Irving L. Janis, and Harold H. Kelley, *Communication and Persuasion* (New Haven: Yale University Press, 1953), p. 11.
5. *Ibid.*, p. 35.

tant for opinion and behavior change. These other factors will be explored in subsequent chapters.

• *The Court in the American Political System*

What are the characteristics of the Court as an originator of messages? First of all, it is perceived as having a legal and constitutional right to do what it does; that is, it is legitimate. The Court partakes of a kind of legitimacy which Weber referred to as legalistic domination stemming from rationally created rules, such as constitutions. Since the Constitution specifically provides for the Court, it is generally recognized that the Court rightfully carries out its obligations. Because of the very intimate relationship between law and the American political system, as manifested by the Constitution itself, one finds a particularly strong basis of legitimacy for the Court.

When a distinction is sought which differentiates our particular governmental form from those of competing types, probably the most frequently noted difference is embodied in the "myth" of a "government of *laws* not of *men*." The word "myth" is used here in a rather specific sense. A "government of laws not of men" is certainly not an empirical statement. It is a fiction, albeit unconscious, which states a goal value, held by society as a whole. The articulation of such a "myth" generates a "unity of feeling"; it evokes a common emotional response in the members of society. Lasswell tells us that

> myth is part of the predisposition that determines response . . . a storehouse of word tools for the political discourse of a community . . . ; it provides a structure of goal values, identifications, and expectations . . . held with varying degrees of elaborations and intensity . . . for society as a whole.[6]

The myth of a "government of laws not of men," then, appears to be one of the most potent of those word tools that link men, one to another, in our society.

The position of the Constitution in our scheme of things is a manifestation of this myth. The Constitution is recognized as higher law, the source from which all other law flows. It sets up the duties and

6. Harold D. Lasswell, Daniel Lerner, and C. Easton Rothwell, *The Comparative Study of Elites* ("Hoover Institute Studies," Ser. C, No. 1) (Stanford: Stanford University Press, 1952).

the limits of authority of the governors in their relationship to the governed. It divides authority between competing loci of power, giving each some checks over the others so that power cannot be concentrated and authority abused. The Constitution, in short, is the device by which idiosyncratic influences can theoretically be held to a minimum in the governing process.

Inasmuch as "law," embodied in the written Constitution, occupies such a pivotal position in our theory, it is understandable that a Court be established as the protector and interpreter of this fundamental law. The Constitution provides for this in part by establishing the judiciary as a coordinate branch of government and granting it a measure of independence by giving the justices lifetime tenure and guaranteeing that they need not fear removal from office by unsympathetic executive or legislative officials. The Court itself complemented the constitutional provisions by assuming the power of "judicial review" of executive and legislative acts. That such a role is popularly perceived as proper may be deduced from the fact that little public disapprobation accompanied the "power grab" by the Court in *Marbury v. Madison.*[7] Continuing public support for the Court in the early New Deal era is a latter-day manifestation of acceptance of this role.

It is a logical development, then, to have a high court interpret the basic dogma—the myth of the supremacy of law—to ensure that modern government is being operated in accordance with the prescriptions of the basic document. In all of this the Court obviously helps strengthen tradition as it views modern happenings in light of the "intentions of the framers." Thus, the Court is an important link with

the "Founding Fathers," which in itself is an important myth and basis for legitimacy.

There are devices which allow us to depreciate the inevitable human element in the administration of justice. The legal realm has a myth which is the counterpart of the basic societal myth discussed above. Jerome Frank labeled it the myth of "legal certainty," which states that "law is, or can be made, unwavering, fixed and settled." [8] This legal myth is given wide currency in the legal profession and has the effect of minimizing the human element involved in adjudication. The law, we are sometimes told, is not made but "discovered." It is some-

7. 1 Cranch 137 (1803).
8. *Law and the Modern Mind* (Garden City: Doubleday & Co., Inc., 1963).

thing which is always there and is merely found by the judge. This argument is often used to counter criticism concerning "judicial legislation."

This desire for a fixed and certain law can be seen in the reliance on *stare decisis.* Since the law is elucidated rather than made by the judges, it is proper that legal rules discovered in an earlier day should apply with equal force to modern situations of a like nature. Although not bound by the doctrine of *stare decisis* to the same extent as judges at common law, the Court nevertheless endeavors to follow what earlier Courts have said. Generally speaking, only with great reluctance will the Court overrule an earlier decision. Rather than overtly to overrule, the Court prefers other devices for getting around an unwanted rule. One of the favorite means is that of the "distinguishing rule," where the Court may point out minute differences in cases. For example, rather than overrule a previous decision outlawing religious education in public schools on school time,[9] the Court distinguished a case involving similar circumstances on the grounds that the religious instruction took place on school time although outside the school buildings.[10] Another favored device is that of "verbal stability," in which the words of old rules are stuffed with new meanings. Finally, a third device, *ratio decidendi,* allows the judge to determine what the "real" meaning of a former decision really is.[11]

One can see the conscious attempt of the Supreme Court to create an aura of stability in its handling of the Constitution in its frequent allusions to the Founding Fathers and the applicability of their views, as if in perpetuity. Chief Justice Taney, for instance, captured this idea in his statement that the Constitution "speaks not only in the same words, but with the same meaning and intent with which it spoke when it came from the hands of the framers." [12]

The "slot-machine" theory of adjudication exemplifies this same quest for stability and certainty. Justice Roberts summarized this theory in a widely quoted passage in *U.S. v. Butler:*

> . . . when an act of Congress is appropriately challenged in the Courts . . . the judicial branch . . . has only one duty,—to lay the article of

9. *Illinois ex rel. McCollum v. Board of Education,* 333 U.S. 203 (1948).
10. *Zorach v. Clauson,* 343 U.S. 306 (1952).
11. All three of these are discussed in Jerome Frank, *Courts on Trial* (Princeton: Princeton University Press, 1950).
12. *Dred Scott v. Sanford,* 19 Howard 393 (1857).

the Constitution which is involved beside the statute which is challenged and to decide whether the latter squared with the former.[13]

The myth of legal certainty, then, provides a convenient means by which the human element is minimized in the judicial process. The judge as policy-maker enjoys a protective insulation not experienced by his colleagues in the other branches of the government.[14] Certain other devices at the disposal of the justices enhance this insulation. First, the Court possesses a large measure of discretion as to which cases it wishes to hear. Through its power to issue writs of certiorari, the Court, by the concurrence of four of its members, may choose to review a lower court's action if so petitioned. The Court possesses less discretionary power in respect to appeals. Nevertheless, the Court does exhibit a measure of discretion on appeals in that it may decide to hear an appeal only if a "substantial" federal question is involved. Such discretion may serve to prevent the Court from hearing cases which could constitute a threat to its authority.

The Court has from time to time articulated rules which ostensibly protect its integrity. The doctrine of the "political question"—where the Court contends that the issue is political in nature, not legal, and that relief consequently lies not in the judiciary but in the "political" branches of government—is one such device. Justice Brandeis conveniently provided a compendium of additional rules adopted by the Court over the years which lessens the necessity for it to involve itself in constitutional matters of a potentially damaging nature. In his concurrence in *Ashwander v. Tennessee Valley Authority,* Brandeis enumerated the following rules:

1. The Court will not pass upon the constitutionality of legislation in a friendly, nonadversary proceeding. . . .
2. The Court will not "anticipate a question of constitutional law in advance of the necessity of deciding it.". . .
3. The Court will not "formulate a rule of constitutional law broader than is required by the precise facts to which it is to be applied.". . .

13. 297 U.S. 1 (1935). The legal profession understandably furthers this conception of legal certainty and the concomitant notion of the depersonalization of the judicial process. See "Canons of Judicial Ethics," Martindale and Hubbell *Law Directory,* Vol. III, pp. 129A–131A, in particular canon 19, "Judicial Opinions"; 20, "Influence of Decisions upon the Development of Law"; and 21, "Idiosyncrasies and Inconsistencies."

14. For a discussion of "judicial insulation" see Jack W. Peltason, *Federal Courts in the Political Process* (Garden City: Doubleday & Co., Inc., 1955), pp. 22–25.

4. The Court will not pass upon a constitutional question, although properly presented by the record, if there is also present some other ground upon which the case may be disposed of. . . .
5. The Court will not pass upon the validity of a statute upon complaint of one who fails to show that he is injured by its operation. . . .
6. The Court will not pass upon the constitutionality of a statute at the instance of one who has availed himself of its benefits. . . .
7. "When the validity of an act of the Congress is drawn in question, and even if a serious doubt of constitutionality is raised, it is a cardinal principle that this Court will first ascertain whether a construction of the statute is fairly possible by which the question may be avoided." [15]

Other means of judicial insulation than those articulated by the Court are operative as well. In a political system characterized by the deep involvement of a multiplicity of special-interest groups acting in very direct and informal ways, it is to be expected that such groups will necessarily approach the Court both through very formal channels and in very indirect ways.[16] Groups may inspire litigation or attempt to present their viewpoint through the *amicus curiae* procedure. Or special interests may attempt to gain access in a rather indirect fashion by striving to influence the recruitment of justices of "proper" thought patterns. All this is true, yet instruments of interpersonal influence widely accepted elsewhere in the governmental system are not sanctioned in the judicial process. It is not considered proper, for instance, to "buttonhole" a justice in order to secure favorable action in a pending case. Nor is it proper for reporters to interview a justice and probe for the "real" reason why he voted in a particular way in a particular case. Judge Medina has clearly indicated that judges, at all levels, are not to be treated as their colleagues in other parts of government normally are. Medina, who was exposed to a great deal of pressure when he presided over the federal district court trial of the eleven top Communists in 1948, emphatically stated that citizens

> . . . should not write letters to a judge who has a matter under advisement, or in any other manner communicate with the judge to tell him how he ought to decide the case. A judge is supposed to reach his decision on the basis of what lawyers and witnesses tell him in the court room,

15. 297 U.S. 288, 345–48.

16. This is discussed in David B. Truman, *The Governmental Process* (New York: Alfred A. Knopf, 1962), Chap. 15.

> not on the basis of private communications which do not form a part of the official record. This business of picketing and deluging a judge with letters and telegrams during a trial is absolutely wrong.[17]

In various ways the human element has been removed from the administration of justice, and the judge is insulated from many of the pressures experienced by others in public life. But the human element is involved. It has the effect of enhancing acceptance of Court policy in certain respects. Viewing the relatively few men named to the high bench, we see a collectivity which is far from representative of the society as a whole. Examination of the backgrounds of the men who have sat on the U.S. Supreme Court in its 175-year history, reveals a remarkable collection of human talent.[18] By mere educational prerequisites alone, the justices are set apart from most other individuals. Not only have all of them had legal training, but most have been the recipients of prestige-university undergraduate training, and many have had graduate training as well. Over a third of the justices have received their undergraduate training in the prestigious Ivy League schools, and over a third did their legal study in those schools.

The modal justice exhibits an economically privileged familial background. Such a background often has allowed the justice the academic advantages which have been a virtual prerequisite for appointment to the Court, as noted above. In addition, Schmidhauser suggests that such a background has instilled in the modal justice a political and social consciousness not characteristic of the present-day American middle class,

> a type which has become increasingly apolitical, interested more in comfort and security than in the assumption of social responsibility. On the contrary, a high percentage of the [justices'] families demonstrated a very deep sense of social responsibility and political involvement . . . ; the biographical data on the justices evidences a considerable conditioning of broad attitudes toward social and political participation.[19]

Public affairs for most people are peripheral.[20] The milieu of which most Supreme Court justices and perhaps judges in general have been

17. Quoted in Peltason, *op. cit.*, p. 22.

18. For an aggregate view of the Court, the source of this material on the background of the justices, see John R. Schmidhauser, *The Supreme Court: Its Politics, Personalities and Procedures* (New York: Holt, Rinehart, & Winston, 1961).

19. *Ibid.*, p. 56.

20. Robert E. Lane, *Political Life* (Glencoe: The Free Press, 1959); Angus Campbell *et al.*, *The American Voter* (New York: John Wiley & Sons, 1960).

a part, however, is one which has enhanced the development of social responsibility, which has in turn led to a political involvement of a very intense kind. The men elevated to the high bench have not been "hothouse" varieties, unused to the exigencies of public life. Rather, the vast majority of the justices have had prior experience in either national or state government.[21] Thus the men who have sat on the U.S. Supreme Court bench have enjoyed a high social status and have exhibited certain educational and experiential traits which have set them apart from the so-called common man. These are additional factors which may make the acceptance of their interpretations somewhat more compelling.

• *Dramaturgy*

Willard Uphaus has related to us his impression of the atmosphere prevailing in the Supreme Court when his appeal was considered.[22] He felt that all was "enveloped by spaciousness and quiet":

> People who attended the hearing stepped lightly and voices were subdued. It seemed that here the harsh, competitive world was shut out and that reason and judgment would prevail. I took a seat with calm and hope in my heart.[23]

In other words, Uphaus was presented with a particular definition of the situation. The United States Supreme Court, although a setting for political conflict, nevertheless suggested to him that the issue at bar would be settled dispassionately and fairly.

The major theme of this chapter has been the unique characteristics of the Supreme Court which set it apart from other institutions in this political system.[24] Certain of these factors are given visible form in the physical environment within which the justices operate and in the particular ways they go about their business and produce the impression described in Uphaus' statement. Erving Goffman has suggested that "any social establishment may be profitably studied from the point

21. S. Sidney Ulmer, "Public Office in the Social Background of Supreme Court Justices," 21 *American Journal of Economics and Sociology* 57 (1962).

22. *Uphaus v. Wyman*, 360 U.S. 72 (1959).

23. Willard Uphaus, *Commitment* (New York: McGraw-Hill, Inc., 1963), p. 2.

24. While the emphasis in this chapter is on the U.S. Supreme Court, it is contended that the formulation is also applicable to most formal courts in this country, whether they be at the national or state level. Courts in general display characteristics—modes of procedure and dress, among other things—which set them apart.

of view of impression management." [25] That is to say, an individual or a team of individuals actively attempt to present to an audience, of one or many, a given definition of the situation. In the case of the Supreme Court—or almost any formal judicial body—the situation is defined as one of fairness, consensus, contemplation, and detachment. This active presentation of a definition of the situation, which Goffman refers to as a "performance," will engage our attention for the next several paragraphs.

Using this notion of performance, we can observe a number of factors which contribute to the definition of the Supreme Court situation. Of initial importance is what may be referred to as "front," i.e., "the expressive equipment of a standard kind intentionally or unwittingly employed by the individual during his performance." [26] Standard parts of the front may be distinguished as between (1) the setting—the physical layout or physical front, and (2) the personal front—the expressive equipment associated with the performer or team of performers personally.

The physical front occupies a strategic position in a Supreme Court performance, as Willard Uphaus' description indicates. When one climbs the innumerable steps leading into the gleaming white marble "palace," he enters a world far removed from his normal everyday experience. The actual performance takes place in the small and rather intimate hearing room. This room, with its Ionic columns, heavy maroon velours draperies, impressively high ceilings, and wooden friezes depicting lawgivers of history and legend, exemplifies stability. The focal point of the room is, of course, the dais with its imposing wooden "bench," behind which the principal performers sit. Interestingly, the justice's chairs are not uniform but rather conform to the individual desires of the justices, a fact suggestive, perhaps, of the independent judgment of the justices themselves. Those who present arguments to the Court occupy a place in the forefront, immediately before the desk, but at a somewhat lower level. Goose-quill pens adorn the desks of these lawyers—impressive evidence of the tradition and permanence of this august institution.

At the stroke of ten a gavel crashes and the Court crier intones: "The Honorable, the Chief Justice and the Associate Justices of the United States." The heavy draperies part and the nine justices enter,

25. Erving Goffman, *The Presentation of Self in Everyday Life* (Garden City: Doubleday & Co., Inc., 1959), p. 238.

26. *Ibid.*, p. 22.

taking their places according to seniority. This presents a new stimulus to the beholder, that which Goffman refers to as "personal front." [27] The mere sight of the justices invokes one set of stimuli comprising personal front—that of appearance. Symbolically, the justices are garbed in black robes, appearing "brushed with divinity," as the late Jerome Frank has commented. The robe exists as a powerful symbol announcing in "impressive terms that the judge is a member of a caste at once mysterious and aristocratic." [28] Certainly, members of the judiciary *are* the only specially garbed public officials and are thus set apart from others who staff the government.

Again the crier intones:

> Oyez! Oyez! Oyez! All persons having business before the Honorable, the Supreme Court of the United States are admonished to draw near and give their attention, for the Court is now sitting! God save the United States and this Honorable Court!

The intonation ushers in another set of stimuli comprising personal front—that of the "manner" of the performers. One views, not nine dissociated actors, but rather a group of justices performing as a "team" to convey the appropriate definition of the situation.[29] The lawyers, in polished prose, present their arguments, while at least some justices dutifully and carefully listen, even though they have had access to the briefs for some time prior to the hearing. Seldom is anything presented in the oral arguments which had not been included in the brief; in fact, the justices disdain such "surprises." And rarely is the advocate permitted to present his argument without interruption, for the justices ask probing questions, ostensibly to penetrate the depths of the issue.

These are the principal performers then: the nine team members and the advocates for the two sides involved in the litigation. At least it is only these, save the crier, who have speaking parts. The Court's clerk and its marshal, attired in cutaway coats, help fill the scene; otherwise they appear to play a small dramaturgical role. Of perhaps a bit more importance are the young page boys, in their black knickerbockers and stockings, whom the justices keep on the run to retrieve

27. *Ibid.*, p. 24.
28. Jerome Frank, *Courts on Trial*, p. 255.
29. Goffman defines a team as "a set of individuals whose intimate co-operation is required if a given projected definition of the situation is to be maintained. A team is a grouping—in relation to an interaction or series of interactions in which the relevant definition of the situation is maintained" (Goffman, *op. cit.*, p. 104).

legal briefs, law reports, and legal tomes.[30] During the arguments some judges are observed in apparent deep study of the materials brought to them.

Of special note is opinion day. The member appointed to speak for the "team" in a particular case announces the decision, reading the majority opinion *in toto* or excerpting from it. John P. Frank, a lawyer intimately familiar with the Court as Hugo Black's one-time law clerk, speaks of this ceremony:

> This is a remarkable proceeding; a busy institution interrupts pressing work to tell a handful of persons in the courtroom what everyone else in the country necessarily learns by reading . . . ; as much as twenty per cent of the courtroom time for a week may go into these statements, all of which would be as effective if the justices simply handed them to the official reporter.[31]

Surely the time spent in opinion-reading is unnecessary insofar as the actual work of the Court is concerned. Frank contends, however, that this procedure is "deeply gratifying" to the beholder and should be among the last elements to be sacrificed to the pressure of time. Certainly from a dramaturgical point of view the formal announcement of the decision is of great importance. This constitutes the denouement of a series of interrelated acts and displays in varying degrees the solidarity of the Court. Not generally evident to the uninitiated observer, significantly, are the costs involved in achieving a consensus among the majority justices.

To be sure, the nine justices do not always achieve unanimity, and opinion day is marked by comments from those who dissent from the majority position. In certain respects this may be viewed as a disruption of the team performance and seen as a noticeable chink in the solidarity of the Court. On the other hand, just as the announcement of the opinion of the Court has been institutionalized, so has the announcement of the dissent. As in the case of the majority opinions, the dissent is usually presented in a calm and decorous manner, regardless of the heat that may have been generated during the deliberations.

At times, to be sure, interjudge conflict comes to light in a dissent,

30. The four Court pages, three whites and a Negro, are hired when they are five feet, one inch tall and are promoted or fired when they reach five feet, six inches; this is apparently the most effective range for their dramaturgical role. For these and other interesting descriptive statements see Paul F. Healy, "Backstage at the Supreme Court," *Saturday Evening Post,* January 20, 1960, pp. 22–23.

31. John P. Frank, *Marble Palace: The Supreme Court in American Life* (New York: Alfred A. Knopf, 1958), p. 121

but this seems to be the exception rather than the rule. The sort of conflict which does emerge is often too subtle to be perceived by the uninitiated audience; as insider John Frank succinctly describes:

> Normally the intra-Court reproaches are made with a gentle touch. A device occasionally used is to quote something one of the Justices has said in another place which appears to conflict with what he is saying in an opinion, as when Justice Jackson searched out observations that Justice Black as Senator Black had made on the floor of the Senate, or when Justice Black dissenting from Justice Frankfurter quoted from a publication of onetime Professor Frankfurter. . . . The thrust and parry of battle is likely to consist of a barbed sentence met by a devastating citation. Instances of public dispute more severe than this are extremely rare.
>
> Far more striking than the Court's disputes over the years is the absence of personal friction among the justices, and the extent to which normal tendencies of irritability are controlled rather than exposed. When one considers how easily a bench of nine could march off in nine different directions, one's principal impression may well be not how often but how seldom this occurs.[32]

Thus the Court over the years has seemed to be cognizant of the desirability of maintaining the positive elements of conflict while attempting to ensure that it does not adversely offset the definition of the situation being generated. The Court has provided for this through the institutionalization of the dissent, which in normal instances is minimally disruptive of the performance, if disruptive at all. Goffman would seem to be directly referring to the dissent procedure when he notes that an

> interaction can be purposely set up as a time and place for voicing differences of opinion, but in such cases participants must be careful to agree not to disagree on the proper tone of voice, vocabulary, and degree of seriousness in which all arguments are to be phrased, and upon the mutual respect which disagreeing participants must carefully continue to express toward one another.[33]

In this sense, then, a compromise is implicitly entered into by the participants. The right of dissent from the majority position is acknowledged, and an institutional procedure is available for this purpose. On the other hand, within this framework a particular *modus*

32. *Ibid.*, pp. 256–59.
33. Goffman, *op. cit.*, p. 10.

operandi is agreed to. This compromise does much to ensure the desired definition of the situation.

The oral argument and the subsequent formal announcement of the decision are the only two visible acts of what is essentially a three-act drama. The second act—the most important one—takes place in what Goffman refers to as the "back region" or "backstage."[34] Here activity takes place which is ancillary to impression management but is absolutely vital to the substantive task of rendering a decision. It is in this region, carefully concealed from the view of the audience, that briefs are reviewed, points of law are researched, cases are discussed, negotiations take place, votes are taken, task assignments are made, and opinions are written. Some of this activity takes place in the office suites of the justices, which are accessible to Court personnel only; the remainder takes place in the sacrosanct conference chamber, which, by tradition, is open only to the justices themselves.

As to what occurs in the conference chamber—where the discussion, negotiation, and voting take place—we are at the mercy of justices who have given us bits and pieces of information. Former Justice James Byrnes has told us that many of the same sort of consensual rules evident in the front region hold backstage as well:

> When the members gather for a conference or for a session of Court, it has been the custom for more than half a century that upon entering the room each should shake hands with all his colleagues, who are referred to as "brethren." On my first day I regarded this as rather superfluous, for I had greeted each of the brethren elsewhere that morning. . . . But I soon realized that it was a useful reminder of the courtesy and mutual respect that the Justices seek to preserve no matter how heated their debates.[35]

We also know that the Chief Justice presides over the conference, summarizing the cases being considered and presenting his own views first. The senior associate justice next offers his position and is followed by the rest according to seniority. The conference is then thrown open to general discussion, which is said in many instances to be lively. On the vote, the most recently appointed justice votes first—allegedly

34. "A back region or backstage may be defined as a place, relative to a given performance, where the impression fostered by the performance is knowingly contradicted as a matter of course" (*ibid.*, p. 112).

35. James F. Byrnes, "The Supreme Court at Work," in Andrew M. Scott and Earle Wallace (eds.), *Politics, U.S.A.* (New York: The Macmillan Co., 1961), p. 45.

so that he will not be influenced by his seniors—followed by his brethren in order of ascending seniority. It is to be emphasized that what we know about these internal procedures has come from the participants themselves, as no one else is permitted entry to the conference. Pages dutifully wait outside the closed doors of the conference chamber for possible assignments. Such assignments are transported to the doors and the waiting auxiliaries by the most recently appointed justice.[36]

Beyond this we know little about what goes on in the inner sanctum or in the office suites of the justices. It is understandable that elaborate precautions are taken to hide this back region from the gaze of the audience. For spirited argument and negotiation between the justices would not necessarily be congruent with the impression of awe, reverence, consensus, and legal certainty being generated in the front region. As long as tensions and bitterness can be kept backstage, the deliberative phase, with its secretive nature, can reinforce the impression engendered up front. Indeed, Chief Justices have expended great effort to curtail controversy even in the back region to ensure a desirable external image. William Howard Taft and Charles Evans Hughes were recognized for their efforts in this regard. Hughes's successor as Chief Justice, Harlan Fiske Stone, was singularly unsuccessful in this regard, and his Court was often accused of neglecting the "theatrical element."[37]

Thus the setting of decision-making emerges as an important consideration in evaluating the Supreme Court as a message source. Clearly

36. Certain scholars have had access to confidential memoranda and have utilized them in publications; see, e.g., Alexander Bickel, *The Unpublished Opinions of Mr. Justice Brandeis: The Supreme Court at Work* (Cambridge: Harvard University Press, 1957), and Alpheus T. Mason, *Harlan Stone: Pillar of the Law* (New York: Viking Press, 1956). John Frank has expressed concern over the use of such material: "But the free give-and-take of a secret conference may dry up if the Justices feel that what may be highly biased accounts by some of their brothers are going to find their way into the history books. The use of confidential notes may make it extremely unlikely that there will be any more confidential notes left around for biographers" (John P. Frank, *op. cit.*, p. 111).

37. "The Justices on Stone's Court, along with the Chief Justice himself, did, in fact, neglect what Walter Bagehot has described as the 'theatrical element.' They were neither mystic in their claims nor occult in action. Without camouflage they attempted to execute the political function of the Supreme Court in a straightforward way. They let it be known, that power and individual conviction decide complex political questions. Law thus shorn of its magic seemed shockingly irreverent to people who preferred to maintain the image of changeless law" (Mason, *op. cit.*, p. 799).

inessential for the resolution of a particular dispute, it is important for dramatizing repeatedly to a relatively uninvolved mass audience the rule of law in the American political system.[38]

Thus Supreme Court justices—through constitutional arrangements, norms of nonapproachability through normal political channels, socioeconomic and political characteristics, and the particular nature of their performance—have been set apart from participants in other branches of government and even more from the mass of the citizenry. These factors combine to provide a very important ingredient for the exercise of authority, namely, "social distance." [39] Because of this distance, the justices are removed from the exigencies of political warfare and political pressures and seemingly can conduct their business in an atmosphere of calm and deliberation. Freed from such exigencies, the justices may focus upon circumstances involved in litigation and reach decisions which are "right" and "proper." "Truth" may be sought without the necessity for accommodating significant others. The Court is allowed, therefore, to take positions on a wide variety of divisive issues—racial integration, church-state controversies, legislative apportionment, the civil liberties of unpopular minorities—which the so-called political branches and political actors, closer to the scene of battle, often cannot think of taking.

The importance of this phenomenon has been suggested in studies of the implementation of the Court's desegregation orders. Jack Peltason, in his study of district court judges in the South, speaks of the Supreme Court as being at the apex of a "hierarchy of scapegoats." In such matters of deep personal concern, a local school board is not as well situated to oppose the local power structure as the United States district court, which in turn is not as well situated as the courts of appeal. Obviously the Supreme Court is in the best situation of all "to take the heat." [40] Consequently, Peltason feels that the Court erred in not giving a more forthright and less ambiguous order in the school-desegregation matter, one which would have allowed school boards to

38. Thurman W. Arnold, in *The Symbols of Government* (New York: Harcourt, Brace & World, Inc., 1962), develops this difference between the general symbolic aspect of the trial and its instrumental aspect of resolving a particular controversy (see esp. Chap. VI, "The Criminal Trial"). Also generally useful on this matter is Murray Edelman, *The Symbolic Uses of Politics* (Urbana: University of Illinois Press, 1964), esp. Chap. 5, "Political Settings as Symbolism."

39. Robert Michels, "Authority," *Encyclopedia of the Social Sciences* (New York: Macmillan, 1930), Vol. II, p. 319.

40. *Fifty-Eight Lonely Men* (New York: Harcourt, Brace & World, 1961), p. 246.

act unequivocally while being able to shift blame upward to this "distant" Court. The Court is in a position to enunciate broad social principles and in turn take the brunt of the criticism when those nearer the scene of battle implement these principles.

Besides being in an unrivaled position to achieve *public compliance* with societal goals even when they may conflict with local mores, the Court can similarly be a catalyst in the achievement of the *private acceptance* of such goals. Changing behavior through legal action—whether by legislative or judicial fiat—can be an important factor in securing attitudinal change as well. Gordon Allport pointed this out when he wrote that "[L]aw is intended only to control the outward expression of intolerance. But outward action, psychology knows, has an eventual effect upon inner habits of thought and feeling." [41] The consequences of messages emanating from the Supreme Court are thus many and immense.

41. Gordon W. Allport, *The Nature of Prejudice* (Garden City: Doubleday & Co., Inc., 1958), p. 442. This point is also made by Morroe Berger, *Equality by Statute* (New York: Columbia University Press, 1952), and Jack W. Brehm and Arthur R. Cohen, *Explorations in Cognitive Dissonance* (New York: John Wiley & Sons, Inc., 1962), esp. Chap. 15, "Applications of Dissonance Theory to Social Problems."

CHAPTER 4

The Messages: "A Wall of Separation"

A COMMUNICATIONS SITUATION, as noted before, may be viewed as presenting certain major classes of stimuli capable of producing incentives leading to the acceptance of the message. We have considered incentives of the first class—those related to the characteristics of the message source—and have argued that certain attributes of the Supreme Court and the way in which it presents itself invoke responses which are congruent with the substance of its policies.

A second class of stimuli deals with the content of the message itself. Messages which are intended to stimulate a desired response from a variety of receivers generally embody certain incentives to assure acceptance and/or compliance. Such incentives may be references to the credibility of the source of the message, arguments substantiating the course of action advocated, positive appeals calling attention to rewards to be gained by acceptance, or negative appeals which point out the unpleasant consequences attendant on noncompliance.[1] We shall now examine the rulings of the Supreme Court which have dealt with religious practices in the public schools, observing the circumstances which have provoked Court action and analyzing the nature of its responses to determine the types of stimuli embodied in its messages.

Since World War II the Supreme Court has on five principal occasions dealt with matters pertaining to religion in public schools.[2]

1. Carl I. Hovland, Irving L. Janis, and Harold H. Kelley, *Communication and Persuasion* (New Haven: Yale University Press, 1953), Chaps. 3 and 4.

2. *Everson v. Board of Education,* 330 U.S. 1 (1947); *Illinois ex rel. McCollum v. Board of Education,* 333 U.S. 203 (1948); *Zorach v. Clauson,* 343 U.S. 306 (1952); *Engel v. Vitale,* 370 U.S. 421 (1962); and *Abington Township School District v. Schempp,* 374 U.S. 203 (1963).

These cases have all been decided within the context of the establishment-of-religion clause of the First Amendment: "Congress shall make no law respecting an establishment of religion." Since public education is the traditional responsibility of state government, the question has involved the application of this clause through the due-process clause of the Fourteenth Amendment, which applies to the states. The first case to be noted, *Everson v. Board of Education*,[3] brought the establishment clause under the aegis of the due-process clause of the Fourteenth. This decision completed the absorption of elements of the First Amendment by the Fourteenth Amendment, a process that had been going on for over two decades.[4]

There are several bases of Supreme Court influence, as noted in Chapter 2. The policy statements themselves may be viewed as efforts by the Court to invoke one or more of these relationships to obtain the desired response by a broad sector of the public. Since the Court has limited coercive power, the message itself is its primary resource for affecting broad social behavior.

One would expect to find in the messages promulgated by the Court, therefore, a variety of cues designed to invoke the expert and legitimate power relationships we have discussed. According to the theory we are developing, the Court, if it expects compliant behavior to result from its policy statements, will include in such statements not only a rational exposition of the policy but cues as to the Court's expert ability to deal with such matters and the appropriateness of its handling them.

An over-all examination of the messages relating to religious exercises in public schools indicates that cues related to certain aspects of the bases of the Court's power are totally lacking. Expertise is a case in point. Nowhere do the messages allude to the fact that the justices are legal experts and that their interpretations of the establishment clause should be accepted on this basis. Indeed, one justice explicitly recognized that the justices were *not* legally equipped to perform the task of drawing the boundaries of the establishment clause. Robert Jackson, concurring in the McCollum case, stated that it was idle

3. Citations for the principal cases have been included in note 2, *supra;* consequently they will not be repeated in subsequent mentionings of the cases unless material is quoted.

4. *Gitlow v. New York,* 268 U.S. 652 (1925) (freedom of speech and press); *De-Jonge v. Oregon,* 299 U.S. 353 (1937) (freedom of assembly); *Cantwell v. Connecticut,* 310 U.S. 296 (1941) (free exercise of religion).

> to pretend that this task is one for which we can find in the Constitution one word to help us as judges to decide where the secular ends and the sectarian begins in education. Nor can we find guidance in any other legal source. It is a matter on which we can find no law but our own prepossessions.[5]

Nor do the messages contain cues as to the legitimacy of the Court for handling such matters. That is, the opinions do not recite that the Court is an appropriate agent for handling such problems. Perhaps it is unnecessary for the Court overtly to provide this sort of cue; however, it is not without precedent. One may point, for instance, to Marshall's opinion in *Marbury v. Madison*,[6] in which he argues that the Court is obviously the appropriate body to interpret the Constitution and to determine the acceptability of actions by other branches. In most cases, however, explicit allusions to the Court's legitimacy are unnecessary, for the source and the message in these instances are inextricably intertwined, and cues as to the legitimacy of the source are implicit.

Legitimacy, as we saw in Chapter 2, has an important dimension which may be distinguished from the source. The object of attitudes of legitimacy may be the substance of the order—its basic "rightness." Certain behavior is directed by the Court because it is intrinsically right and proper, and acceptance of this position is sought through persuasive argumentation. This "content legitimacy," as an examination of the relevant opinions indicates, is the dominant characteristic of the Court's treatment of the religion-in-public-schools issue. We shall now view the relevant cases in chronological order with these considerations in mind. While the later cases are of more relevance for our purposes here, we shall see that much of the formulation of the Court's position, as well as the rhetoric embodying the position, had its origin in the early cases.

• *Everson v. Board of Education*

In this case, a New Jersey law and a township school-board resolution enacted in pursuance thereof were challenged. The law authorized local school districts to make rules and contracts for the transportation of their children to and from school. The township board, in accordance with the statute, authorized the reimbursement of parents

5. 333 U.S. at 237, 238.
6. 1 Cranch 137 (1803).

who sent their children to schools on buses operated by public transportation systems. Such reimbursement was not confined to parents of public school children, but it was extended to parents of parochial school children as well. Appellants contended, among other things, that this practice constituted the use of state power to support church schools and was thereby prohibited as an establishment of religion.

With Hugo Black writing for the five-man majority, the Supreme Court upheld the school-board's program on the grounds that the state law was to benefit all of its citizens and should not be construed so as to penalize some because of their religious beliefs. State aid was extended to the child and his parents but not for the furtherance of any particular religious creed. Of more importance to us here is the general effect given by Black to the establishment clause:

> The "establishment of religion" clause of the First Amendment means at least this: Neither a State nor the Federal Government can set up a church. Neither can pass laws which aid one religion, aid all religions, or prefer one religion over another. Neither can force nor influence a person to go to or to remain away from church against his will or force him to profess a belief or disbelief in any religion. No person can be punished for entertaining or professing religious beliefs or disbeliefs, for church attendance or non-attendance. No tax in any amount, large or small, can be levied to support any religious activities or institutions, whatever they may be called, or whatever form they may adopt to teach or practice religion. Neither a state nor the Federal Government can, openly or secretly, participate in the affairs of any religious organizations or groups *and* vice-versa. In the words of Jefferson, the clause against establishment of religion by law was intended to erect "a wall of separation between Church and State." [7]

This passage is quoted at length, for it represents a common thread running through each of the subsequent decisions save one.

How does Black come to this conclusion? His entire argument is built on the historical setting in which the words of the establishment clause were framed:

> These words of the First Amendment reflected in the minds of early Americans a vivid mental picture of conditions and practices which they fervently wished to stamp out in order to preserve liberty for themselves and for their posterity.[8]

7. 330 U.S. at 15, 16.
8. *Ibid.*, p. 8.

He then painstakingly delineates the history of church-state relations, beginning with the European experience of our forefathers, who knew a coerced faith and compulsory church attendance as well as the "turmoil," "civil strife," and "persecution" which attended the religious and political linkages of the time.[9] The Colonial experiences were also detailed, showing how these practices were transplanted here—how individuals were "fined, cast in jail, cruelly tortured, and killed" for opposition to the predominant religious group in the colony.[10]

Such practices "shocked" the "freedom-loving colonials into a feeling of abhorrence." [11] This was dramatically the case in Virginia, where James Madison wrote his famous *Memorial and Remonstrance* in opposition to the Assessment Bill, which would have levied a tax to support an established church. Thomas Jefferson shared this leadership against established religions, authoring the "Virginia Bill for Religious Liberty." These men, according to Black, recognized the dangers and persuaded their fellow Virginians that a "true religion did not need the support of law . . . ; that the best interest of a society required that the minds of men always be wholly free." [12]

The nature of the argument is quite clear. The precedents cited were not from the hands of previous judges; rather they were derived from the history of the nation. The quotations from Black suggest that he used a "fear-producing appeal": there were great evils associated with previous experiences with established religions. This fear is underscored and legitimized by the acknowledgment of similar fears on the part of two of the Founding Fathers, Jefferson and Madison. Thus there is an allusion to what has been referred to as the "miranda" of politics—the symbols of sentiment and identification held in common by a people who share certain "fundamental assumptions" about political affairs.[13]

This was a five-to-four decision, but the dispute was not over the

9. *Ibid.*
10. *Ibid.*, p. 9.
11. *Ibid.*, p. 11.
12. *Ibid.*, p. 12.
13. Harold D. Lasswell, Nathan Leites, *et al.*, *The Language of Politics* (New York: George W. Stewart, Inc., 1949), pp. 9–14. See also in this regard Lasswell and Abraham Kaplan, *Power and Society: A Framework for Political Inquiry* (New Haven: Yale University Press, 1950), and Charles E. Merriam, *Political Power* (New York: Whittlesey House, 1934), Chap. II, "The Credenda and Miranda of Power."

interpretation of "establishment of religion." The Court was in unanimity in this regard. The dispute was over the application of the general rule to the precise set of circumstances presented to them, four justices feeling that the New Jersey program should fall because it contravened the First Amendment. Rutledge's dissent, which was concurred in by the three other dissenters, paralleled Black's opinion for the Court in that his argument regarding the meaning of an establishment of religion was based wholly upon historical experience:

> No provision of the Constitution is more closely tied to or given content by its generating history than the religious clause of the First Amendment. It is at once the refined product and the terse summation of that history.[14]

The dissent is a skillful interweaving of Madisonian thought as expressed in *Memorial and Remonstrance* with the New Jersey situation then before the Court.

• *Illinois ex rel. McCollum v. Board of Education*

Close on the heels of the *Everson* case came one which stimulated much public controversy. This case involved the constitutional validity of a program of religious education in the schools of Champaign, Illinois. Here teachers representing private religious groups were allowed to come into the school buildings weekly and conduct classes during regular school hours. Those children not desiring such instruction were not released from school but were sent elsewhere in the building to pursue regular secular studies. The Champaign program was one of many such programs popular at the time.[15] This arrangement was again viewed by Black, for the eight-man majority, as "beyond all question a utilization of the tax-established and tax-supported public school system to aid religious groups to spread their faith." [16] The majority opinion consisted primarily of applying the *Everson* rule to the immediate circumstances and finding that here there was not the required degree of separation. Felix Frankfurter added an extensive

14. 330 U.S. at 33.
15. For an extensive treatment of this movement and a summary of reactions to the *McCollum* decision see Gordon M. Patric, *The Impact of the McCollum Decision Particularly in Illinois,* unpublished doctoral dissertation, University of Illinois, 1957. For a shorter version see 6 *Journal of Public Law* 455 (1957).
16. 333 U.S. at 210.

concurring opinion in which he traced the history of religious education in this country and attempted to illustrate that it was early established that the public schools were to be agents of cohesion in this nation of diverse peoples and that they had to be kept free from the divisiveness of religious sects.[17]

The lone dissenter, Stanley Reed, charged that the majority gave an excessive interpretation to "establishment of religion"; what was prohibited, he said, was the outright establishment of a state-recognized and financed church, and to validate his position he drew upon the same historical data as the majority. Of particular importance was Reed's recitation of a list of practices which evidence a historic closeness between church and state in this nation: the presence of chaplains in the Congress and the military, regular invocations of divine blessings at government functions, government financing for training war veterans for the ministry, and opening exercises in the schools of the District of Columbia which "include a reading from the Bible without note or comment, and the Lord's prayer." [18] This line of argument was to be re-echoed in later Court decisions as well as in the public debate which accompanied them.

The widespread public discussion generated by the Court's decision in the *McCollum* case received "judicial notice" by Hugo Black in his dissenting opinion in the next relevant case, *Zorach v. Clauson,* in 1952:

> I am aware that our *McCollum* decision on separation of church and state has been subjected to a most searching examination throughout the country. Probably few opinions from this Court in recent years have attracted more attention or stirred wider debate. Our insistence on a "wall between church and state which must be kept high and impregnable" has seemed to some a correct exposition of the philosophy and a true interpretation of the language of the First Amendment to which we should strictly adhere. With equal conviction and sincerity, others have thought the *McCollum* decision fundamentally wrong and have pledged continuous warfare against it.[19]

Forces which had viewed the *McCollum* decision with alarm could take comfort in the result of the *Zorach* decision and the language in which it was framed.

17. *Ibid.,* pp. 212–32. For an interesting account by the principal participant in this case see Vashti McCollum, *One Woman's Fight* (Boston: Beacon Press, 1961).
18. 333 U.S. at 254.
19. 343 U.S. at 317.

• *Zorach v. Clauson*

This case involved a "released-time" program of religious education sponsored by the New York public school system. Under this arrangement the public schools released students during regular school hours to leave the school grounds to attend religious instruction or devotional exercises in nearby centers maintained by a variety of religious groups. Those who were not released, upon written request of their parents, were required to stay in their classrooms. Unlike the Champaign, Illinois, program, the physical facilities of the public schools were not utilized. School time was the single accommodation made by the public schools. The appellants, however, contended that the mechanism of compulsory education was instrumental in the support of these religious programs.

William O. Douglas, writing for a six-man majority, acknowledged that the Court was again following the "wall-of-separation" conception of the First Amendment as stated in the two earlier cases. On this occasion, however, the schooltime religious-instruction program was upheld. "The First Amendment," wrote Douglas, ". . . does not say that in every and all respects there shall be separation of Church and State. Rather, it studiously defines the manner, the specific ways, in which there shall be no concert or union or dependency one on the other." [20] He then proceeded to delineate the instances in which there has not been an absolute separation of church and state in America, citing, in addition to the practices earlier noted by Reed, police and fire protection for religious groups by municipalities, traditional Thanksgiving Day proclamations, allusions to the Almighty in messages of the Presidents, the "So help me God" pervasively used in courtroom oaths, and numerous other religiously oriented rituals and ceremonies associated with the state. His final clinching point is an interesting one: "[A] fastidious atheist or agnostic could even object to the supplication with which the Court opens each session: 'God save the United States and this Honorable Court.' " [21]

Douglas' opinion is also especially noteworthy for dicta which have become a rallying point for forces opposed to the Court's policies concerning church-state separation:

> We are a religious people whose institutions presuppose a Supreme Being. We guarantee the freedom to worship as one chooses. We make

20. *Ibid.*, p. 312.
21. *Ibid.*, p. 313.

room for as wide a variety of beliefs and creeds as the spiritual needs of man deem necessary. We sponsor an attitude on the part of government that shows no partiality to any one group and that lets each flourish according to the zeal of its adherents and the appeal of its dogma. When the state encourages religious instruction or cooperates with religious authorities by adjusting the schedule of public events to sectarian needs, it follows the best of our traditions. For it then respects the religious nature of our people and accommodates the public service to their spiritual needs. To hold that it may not would be to find in the Constitution a requirement that the government show a callous indifference to religious groups.[22]

These were the compelling points of argument sustaining the released-time program, and they injected the weekday religious-training movement with new hope.[23] The dissenters could not distinguish this case from others and again cited the dangers inherent in church-state relationships.

• *Engel v. Vitale*

The Court was not to deal with such problems for another decade. In 1962, the constitutionality of the following New York State Board of Regents prayer was questioned:

> Almighty God, we acknowledge our dependence upon Thee, and we beg Thy blessings upon us, our parents, our teachers and our Country.

The prayer was adopted by the Board of Education of New Hyde Park, New York, among others, upon supplication of the State Board of Regents, which had composed the prayer. The Court, in a six-to-one decision, reinvoked the *Everson* "wall of separation" interpretation and found the state laws requiring or permitting the use of the Regents' prayer to be violative of the Constitution.

Writing once again for the majority, Hugo Black drew mainly on historical materials to strike down the prayer. He detailed the struggles in England attending the adoption of the Book of Common Prayer and its subsequent amendments. Similar religious struggles in the

22. *Ibid.*, pp. 313, 314.

23. For a general treatment of the *Zorach* case see Frank J. Sorauf, "The Released Time Case," in C. Herman Pritchett and Alan F. Westin (eds.), *The Third Branch of Government* (New York: Harcourt, Brace & World, Inc., 1963), pp. 118–48. For a more detailed analysis of the impact of *Zorach* see Sorauf, "*Zorach v. Clauson:* The Impact of a Supreme Court Decision," 53 *American Political Science Review* 777 (1959).

Colonies precipitated Madison's and Jefferson's intense opposition to an established church. The framers saw to it that these common experiences were reflected in the First Amendment to preclude the "anguish," "hardship," and "bitter strife" which are the concomitants of an established religion.[24] Black's argument, as well as the symbols he used, was reminiscent of the *Everson* opinion.

Black wrote that the First Amendment was not formulated to destroy either religion or prayer. Instead it reflected on the part of its drafters an

> awareness that governments of the past had shackled men's tongues to make them speak only the religious thoughts that government wanted them to speak, and to pray only to God that government wanted them to pray to. It is neither sacrilegious nor antireligious to say that each separate government in this country should stay out of the business of writing or sanctioning official prayers and leave that purely religious function to the people themselves and to those the people choose to look to for religious guidance.[25]

Interestingly, the majority opinion was entirely devoid of citations.

From past experience, Black recognized that this decision would possibly be expanded and perceived by many to evidence a hostility on the part of the Court to religion and prayer in general and to constitute a threat to public recognition of the nation's religious heritage. Perhaps to quell this sort of criticism and fear, Black affixed the following footnote toward the end of the opinion:

> There is of course nothing in the decision reached here that is inconsistent with the fact that school children and others are officially encouraged to express love for our country by reciting historical documents such as the Declaration of Independence which contain references to the Deity or by singing officially espoused anthems which include the composer's professions of faith in a Supreme Being, or with the fact that there are many manifestations in our public life of belief in God. Such patriotic or ceremonial occasions bear no true resemblance to the unquestioned religious exercise that the State of New York has sponsored in this instance.[26]

The importance of this footnote will be seen later on.

William O. Douglas wrote a concurring opinion in which he was primarily concerned with the matter of government financing of

24. 370 U.S. at 429.
25. *Ibid.,* p. 435.
26. *Ibid.*

religious exercises. Although lacking in clarity, his opinion seems to indicate that the Constitution forbids such financing by the government and that consequently the New York program must fall. He goes beyond this, however, to liken the New York program to other religious practices evident in public life: prayers by the House and Senate chaplains and the crier's supplication at the opening of the Court. For him, "the principle is the same, no matter how briefly the prayer is said, for in each of the instances given the person praying is a public official on the public payroll, performing a religious exercise in a governmental institution." [27] It is understandable that Douglas' concurring opinion did not enhance the acceptance of the decision.

Potter Stewart, the lone dissenter, refused to agree that "an 'official religion' is established by letting those who want to say a prayer say it." [28] The history presented by the majority was in the main irrelevant, to his way of thinking, while the long tradition of church-state cooperation was of great relevance. He picked up the strain, developed earlier by Reed in *McCollum* and Douglas in *Zorach,* in which many instances of state-recognized religious practices are enumerated. The Regents' Prayer was viewed as mere additional evidence of the "deeply entrenched and highly cherished spiritual traditions of our nation." [29]

• *Abington Township School District v. Schempp*

One year later, on the final day of the 1962–63 term, Justice Tom Clark announced the most recent decision in this series. This decision handled two companion cases which differed in factual nature but which the Court felt allowed joint treatment. In one a 1959 Pennsylvania statute was being challenged which provided that "at least ten verses from the Holy Bible should be read at the opening of each public school day." [30] The law permitted school children to be excused upon the written request of their parents or guardians. The district court for the Eastern District of Maryland, on petition of a Unitarian family, found the Pennsylvania statute violative of the establishment clause. In the other case [31] the Maryland Court of Appeals, on petition of an atheistic mother and her son of like beliefs, sustained the ruling of

27. *Ibid.,* p. 441.
28. *Ibid.,* p. 445.
29. *Ibid.,* p. 450.
30. 24 Pennsylvania Statute. Sec. 15-1516 as amended, Public Law 1928 (Supp. 1960), Dec. 17, 1959.
31. *Murray v. Curlett,* 228 Md. 239, 179 A 2d 698.

the trial court, which had upheld a rule of the School Commissioners of Baltimore City providing for opening devotional exercises in the public schools of the city. These exercises included the "reading, without comment, of a chapter in the Holy Bible and/or the use of the Lord's Prayer." [32] The Court, through Tom Clark, affirmed the Pennsylvania district court ruling and reversed that of the Maryland Court of Appeals. Thus the Court refused approval to programs providing for these specific religious practices in the public schools.

Insofar as form is concerned, the majority opinion in *Schempp* departs markedly from those which had preceded it. While the prior opinions had been primarily historical exigeses, largely devoid of legal precedents, this decision abounds with case citations and quotations, as Table 1 illustrates.

TABLE 1

Precedent Cases Cited in *Abington Township School District v. Schempp*

Precedent Cases	Times Cited	Lines Quoted
Everson	7	78
McCollum	3	22
Zorach	5	25
McGowan [a]	5	9
Torcaso [b]	4	12
Engel	4	46
Others [c]	5	40
Total	33	232

[a] *McGowan v. Maryland*, 366 U.S. 420 (1961), Sunday-closing-law case.

[b] *Torcaso v. Watkins*, 367 U.S. 488 (1961), religious-test-oath case.

[c] *Minor v. Board of Education*, Superior Court of Cincinnati, 1870 (1); *Cantwell v. Connecticut*, 310 U.S. 296 (1940) (2); *Murdock v. Pennsylvania*, 319 U.S. 105 (1943) (1); *West Virginia State Board of Education v. Barnette*, 319 U.S. 624 (1943) (1). These four cases involved primarily the free-exercise-of-religion clause of the First Amendment.

Since four pages of a thirteen-page majority opinion were devoted to a statement of the facts involved in the two cases and nearly two pages more consisted of footnotes, it is readily apparent that the thirty-three

32. Board of School Commissioners of Baltimore City pursuant to Art. 77, Sec. 202, of the Annotated Code of Maryland, 1905, as amended.

case citations and a total of over two pages of quotations therefrom occupied a significant portion of the opinion.

As with the precedent decisions, *Schempp* again placed important emphasis on the historical argument pointing to the serious disadvantages attendant upon church-state ties. Instead of presenting an original treatment of the history, Clark pointed out that authority for the Court's stand in this instance was not to be found in documentary evidence nor in the works of scholars of history but rather in the Court's views of the historical element in earlier decisions. Drawing together the diverse threads of the Court's treatment of the establishment clause, Clark was able to formulate an inclusive test:

> As we have indicated, the Establishment Clause has been directly considered by this Court eight times in the past score of years and, with only one Justice dissenting on the point, it has consistently held that the clause withdrew all legislative power respecting religious belief or the expression thereof. The test may be stated as follows: what are the purpose and the primary effect of the enactment? If either is the advancement or inhibition of religion then the enactment exceeds the scope of legislative power as circumscribed by the Constitution. That is to say that to withstand the strictures of the Establishment Clause there must be a secular legislative purpose and a primary effect that neither advances nor inhibits religion.[33]

That the *Schempp* opinion is a summary of the Court's position over the years is quite obvious. Clark combined such opposing opinions as those of *Zorach* and *Engel* to paint a picture of judicial consistency but recognized that the substance involved in such consistency, however, is incomprehensible and troublesome to many. Like Douglas and Black before him, he acknowledged the close traditional ties between church and state in America and went on to include the following statement in the text of the opinion, whereas Black had relegated a similar statement to a footnote:

> The place of religion in our society is an exalted one, achieved through a long tradition of reliance on the home, the church and the inviolable citadel of the individual heart and mind. We have come to recognize through bitter experience that it is not within the power of government to invade that citadel, whether its purpose or effect be to aid or oppose, to advance or retard.[34]

33. 374 U.S. at 222.
34. *Ibid.*, p. 226.

At another point Clark seems to give assurances to those who might question the boundaries of the Court's development of the principle of church-state separation:

> . . . it might well be said that one's education is not complete without a study of comparative religion or the history of religion and its relationship to the advancement of civilization. It certainly may be said that the Bible is worthy of study for its literary and historic qualities. Nothing we have said here indicates that such study of the Bible or of religion, when presented objectively as part of a secular program of education, may not be effected consistent with the First Amendment.[35]

Separate concurring opinions were forthcoming from Arthur Goldberg, the Court's only Jew, and from William Brennan, the Court's only Catholic; the latter's opinion was quite extensive, covering some seventy-four pages, with an elaborate discussion of the various facets involved.[36] Potter Stewart again was alone in dissent, and in this instance his dissent also was very extensive; while he generally disagreed with the Court's application of the establishment-of-religion clause in this as well as earlier cases, his principal point was that coercion to participate in religious exercises had to be shown. The record, Stewart contended, was deficient in this regard, as it failed to show either the presence or absence of coercion in the program. In the absence of such evidence, he felt the program could be sustained.[37]

This more detailed discussion of the relevant cases is intended to substantiate the point made early in the chapter that compliant behavior was sought by the Court through what may be called "content legitimacy." That is to say, the cues provided in these messages did not have to do with the sanctions the Court had at its disposal, to its legal expertise, or to the appropriateness of the Court to settle such questions. Rather, influence was sought through persuasive argumentation. The "miranda" of politics were invoked; the thinking of the Founding Fathers, Madison and Jefferson in particular, was given prominence, showing that modern interpretation of the principles involved was congruent with their original formulation. Historical data were also drawn upon to demonstrate the dangers inherent in church-state collaboration. In three of the cases it was suggested that continuation of the ongoing practices could result in the same sort of strife and damage to both religion and state which our forefathers knew from experience.

35. *Ibid.*, p. 225.
36. *Ibid.*, pp. 230–304.
37. *Ibid.*, pp. 308–20.

Finally, there were allusions, both explicit and implicit, to the rewards to be gained by the acceptance of the Court's policies: a stronger church and a more effective state.

On the other hand, none of the cases drew a unanimous response from the Court. In each case the dissenter was also able to present persuasive arguments in support of an opposed outcome. Consequently, those who disagree with the handling of the cases by the majority obtain a measure of support for their contrary position. This was evident in interviews with individuals in Eastville and Westville. On more than one occasion, persons who disagreed with the majority position pointed out that not even the Court itself was in unanimity. In this sense, then, a dissenting opinion can—like a majority opinion—exist as a symbol to legitimize one's position, and it may be dysfunctional as far as stimulation of compliant behavior and attitudinal change is concerned.

The Court's treatment, even apart from the dissents, could similarly be used to justify other than strictly compliant responses. Although the Court announced a rather rigid "wall of separation" policy in *Everson,* it nevertheless "differentiated" the program involved there from the sort of program which is unacceptable. Again in *Zorach,* while the Court paid lip service to the *Everson-McCollum* doctrine, it found it convenient to distinguish the released-time program of New York from a similar program declared unconstitutional in *McCollum.* Here again, a response alternative to compliance is actually legitimized by the Court's own action.

One additional characteristic of these messages should be noted, namely, the recognition on the part of the Court of the emotional nature of these cases and of the necessity for some symbolic reassurance to allay the antagonisms which might ensue. In three of the five cases the Court took a position counter to the religious practice involved.[38] As discussed above, the *McCollum* decision denied not only instrumental rewards to the religionist but also symbolic rewards as well, as the strict *Everson* "wall of separation" formula was strictly applied. This stimulated widespread antagonism, as evidenced by Black's dissent in *Zorach* and substantiated by Patric's research.[39] Four years later, in *Zorach v. Clauson,* an instrumental reward as well as a strong symbolic reward was accorded to the religionist position.

38. In *McCollum,* the religious-education program; *Engel,* the Regents' Prayer; and *Schempp,* the prescribed Bible reading and Lord's Prayer.

39. Gordon Patric, *op. cit.*

In *Engel* instrumental rewards were denied the religionists, although a rather weak symbolic reward was embodied in the form of a footnote by Black, which was quoted above. The *Engel* decision was received throughout the nation with much genuine concern, while the Black footnote was not given wide attention. One year later, in *Schempp,* the religionist position was again denied instrumental rewards, but this time, even though the decision has broader implications than *Engel,* the decision was received with considerably less antagonism. Here, however, the symbolic reward was given greater prominence in the majority opinion and wider play in the channels through which decisions are transmitted. Thus we see the importance of symbolic rewards in Supreme Court opinions when instrumental rewards are denied in instances of broad social concern. This observation is supported by Murray Edelman's findings and hypotheses regarding substantive and symbolic allocation of resources in the regulatory process.[40]

40. Murray Edelman, "Symbols and Political Quiescence," 54 *American Political Science Review* 695 (1960).

CHAPTER 5

Transmission: The Formal Channels

THE RESULT OF A CASE is announced in the formal setting on opinion day. This is a particularly important part of the drama, as noted in Chapter 3. It is the denouement; the audience is finally apprised of what has taken place backstage. The author of the majority opinion reads it in its entirety, exerpts from it, or summarizes the Court's position. With its official promulgation, the policy becomes binding upon the courts of the land.

To whom is the message addressed? This is not a simple question. Certainly it is immediately addressed to the principals involved in the suit. It specifies or enjoins certain acts on the part of those involved. But much of an opinion is devoted to the explication of a general rule, and the impact of the policy has a temporal and lateral extension far beyond the confines of the specific case involved. Since the Supreme Court stands atop the judicial hierarchy in this country, lower courts of both national and state origin are expected to follow the high court's lead when they are called upon to resolve controversies in which such policy would be applicable.

Radiating out beyond this, a multiplicity of roles are involved, both political and nonpolitical, and those occupying these roles are under some obligation to follow the Court's determinations. With respect to the religion-in-public-schools issue, not only do judges play important roles, but so do state attorneys general, superintendents of public instruction, school superintendents, principals, teachers, and school-board members. Each of these role-players has taken an oath to "support and defend the Constitution of the United States," which presumably entails giving effect to Supreme Court interpretations of the Constitution if the circumstances arise within their respective jurisdictions. Supreme Court messages, while addressed to specific instances and principals, nevertheless reach outward to affect target roles which in turn may give wider scope to the rulings.[1]

In practice, however, the fulfillment of the obligation of compliance is often not very clear-cut. To be sure, the general obligation is clear, but the activity resulting from such an obligation may take many forms. How the general rule will be applied to a particular set of circumstances may vary greatly from actor to actor and community to community. This ambiguity of *who should do what* may be a source of consternation or a convenient "out," depending on one's basic orientation toward the Court's policy. Frank Sorauf is on point when he observes that interests on both sides of the issue perceive the Court's decisions within distinct frames of reference. What views one takes of these precedents and their applicability to ongoing processes "seems to depend on the commitments one brings to his appraisal of the decision." [2]

If a communicator is interested in affecting the behavior of others, clearly it is helpful to convey the expectations in as unambiguous terms as possible. If the messages are clouded with ambiguity, and if those who must take action to implement the message are numerous and loosely coordinated at best, it is likely that the final result will be ambiguous as well. The content elements of Supreme Court decisions, therefore, are particularly important because the lines of influence are so circuitous and tenuous from the Supreme Court as the originator of the messages to those actors who will transform the message into concrete public policy.

That message clarity is an important factor involved in the compliance process is well documented.[3] Unless the message clearly states the expectations for actors at the level of implementation, the chances for behavior congruent with the policy may be very slight, depending upon the local setting. The content elements of the message comprise just one aspect of this problem, however. Another aspect involves the adequacy of the channels through which the messages are transmitted to the points of implementation. The primary point to be made in this chapter and the next is that the adequacy of transmission is an

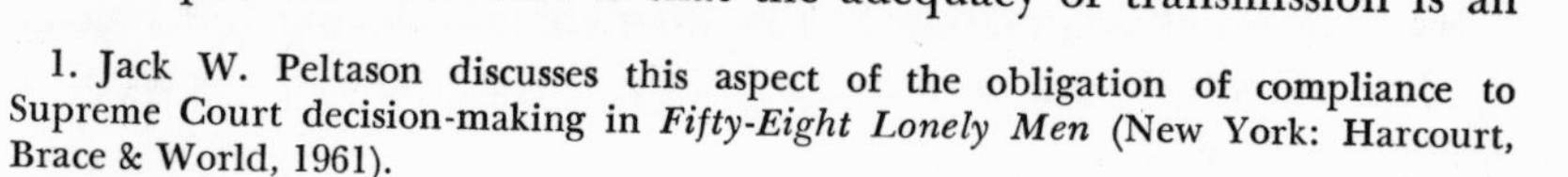

1. Jack W. Peltason discusses this aspect of the obligation of compliance to Supreme Court decision-making in *Fifty-Eight Lonely Men* (New York: Harcourt, Brace & World, 1961).

2. Frank J. Sorauf, "*Zorach v. Clauson:* The Impact of a Supreme Court Decision," 53 *American Political Science Review* 782 (1959).

3. The cited works of Peltason, Sorauf, and Patric point to this important consideration.

important variable in this decisional situation, for behavior congruent with the message depends in large measure upon whether the ruling is received in a relatively undistorted state by those who are affected by it.

Two questions may be asked in this regard: What are the relevant channels of transmission? And what substantive treatment was given to the Court's messages concerning religious practices in public schools? The first question will occupy us in this chapter as we view certain formal channels of transmission. In Chapter 6 we shall focus directly upon the Eastville-Westville district and discuss more relevant channels for this locale of implementation as well as the substantive treatment given to the messages by such transmitters.

• *Formal Legal Channels*

Supreme Court decisions are responses to specific sets of circumstances, and certain behavior is directed to be taken on the part of one or more of the principals involved in the suit. Since the bulk of the work of the Supreme Court is of an appellate nature, cases accepted for review by the Court, either through appeal or certiorari processes, have been heard in lower federal or state courts. In making a final determination in a case, the Supreme Court may remand it to an inferior court for action consistent with the decision. The inferior court may then further transmit the order through formal channels to appropriate bodies for action.

The *McCollum* case may be used as a paradigm to observe the transmission phase of the decisional process when the specific circumstances of a case have come under the scrutiny of the high court. In this instance, the case had come up through the Illinois courts, and a ruling by the Illinois Supreme Court was appealed to the U.S. Supreme Court. Finding contrary to the ruling of the Illinois courts, the Supreme Court remanded the case to the highest state court for action in accordance with its ruling. The Illinois Supreme Court then transmitted an order to the sixth circuit court of Champaign County, the court of original jurisdiction in this case, containing the full text of the *McCollum* ruling as well as the following statement by the clerk of the high state court:

> It is Hereby Ordered by this Court that the judgment of the Circuit Court of Champaign County, Illinois be reversed and the cause remanded to said circuit court for proceedings not inconsistent with the opinion of

the Supreme Court of the United States, a copy of which opinion is annexed hereto and transmitted herewith.[4]

The circuit court further transmitted the ruling, via a writ of mandamus delivered by a deputy sheriff acting as an agent of the court, to the defendant school board. The writ ordered the board to

> immediately adopt and enforce rules and regulations prohibiting all instruction in and teaching of religious education in the manner heretofore conducted by said School District Number 71 in all public schools within the original School District Number 71, Champaign County, Illinois and in all school houses and buildings in said district when occupied by public schools; and . . . to prohibit within said original School District Number 71 the use of the State's public school machinery to help enroll pupils in the several religious classes of sectarian groups.[5]

The formal judicial structure, then, provides an important channel through which a ruling is transmitted to those who are directly under obligation to act. It is in this way that official actors in the legal system are able to observe whether or not compliant behavior ensues and, if it does not, to instigate further legal action against the noncompliant. It is in this respect that the coercive-power relationship may be established.

The decisions themselves are officially published in volumes entitled *United States Reports*, which serve more of a storage function than a direct transmission function. Parallel to these official reports are the privately published reports, *The Supreme Court Reporter* and the *Lawyer's Edition*. These are quite important, as the cases contained in them are frequently cited as precedents and are used to buttress arguments in later cases. Individuals specially trained in the law draw upon this stored information insofar as it has bearing on their immediate concerns. Lawyers and judges are thus important transmitters of Supreme Court decisions.

Just because highly trained individuals transmit Supreme Court decisions through application in later litigation, it does not necessarily follow that all pertinent precedents are noted. Nor does it follow that

4. Illinois Supreme Court, *Order No. 29678* in the case of *Illinois ex rel. McCollum v. Board of Education of School District Number 71*. Case number 18101 in the Office of the Clerk of the Champaign County Court, the Sixth Circuit, filed May 25, 1948, by George W. Temple, Clerk of Court.

5. Illinois Sixth Circuit Court, *Writ of Mandamus* issued in the *McCollum* Case, Number 18101, filed by George W. Temple, Clerk of Court, in the Court Records on September 29, 1948.

precedents, even if applied, are applied in a uniform way throughout the system. John P. Frank notes that lower-court judges do not carry in their heads the substance of over 370 volumes of *United States Reports*, "nor do they commonly stand anxiously at the mail box to receive the new wisdom ground out weekly." [6] If counsel does not call such cases to the judge's attention, the latter might not know the relevant cases that exist. Sorauf makes a similar point. He notes that, after the 1952 *Zorach v. Clauson* decision, lower courts on occasion continued to apply the *McCollum* ruling, even though the *Zorach* precedent seemed more pertinent.[7]

In addition to the ignorance factor, an additional factor of selective interpretation and application may be noted. The rationale asserted to be controlling by the Supreme Court from its exalted vantage point is often viewed quite unsympathetically by district or state court judges, who exist in a radically different milieu. State court and lower federal court judges are, in the main, products of the communities in which their courts are located. They have lived there and have been educated in local schools and generally in the state university and law school; they have strong personal ties in the community and frequently have been active partisans in the political activities of the state and locality.[8] The points we made previously concerning message ambiguity are again relevant. If the message from above is ambiguous, district and state judges will find many convenient openings, allowing them to hand down decisions which will not fly in the face of local values. The transmitters involved, whatever their formal political or legal role, are individuals whose values may be quite different from the values of those who originated the order and who are also subject to different pressures. In short, the formal legal channels through which decisions

6. John P. Frank, *Marble Palace: The Supreme Court in American Public Life* (New York: Alfred A. Knopf, 1958), p. 22.

7. Sorauf, *op. cit.*

8. As opposed to the more or less cosmopolitan backgrounds of the Supreme Court justices as noted in Chapter 3 and in John R. Schmidhauser, *The Supreme Court: Its Politics, Personalities, and Procedures* (New York: Holt, Rinehart, & Winston, 1961), and S. Sidney Ulmer, "Public Office in the Social Background of Supreme Court Justices," 21 *American Journal of Economics and Sociology* 57 (1962), judges in the lower branches of the federal judiciary are more representative of the local community. See Peltason, *op. cit.*, particularly Chapters 1 and 9, and Jack Greenberg, *Race Relations and American Law* (New York: Columbia University Press, 1959), Chapter 1, for statements of this point, particularly as related to the school-desegregation rulings. This picture of the lower federal judiciary is also affirmed by this author's unpublished study of John Kennedy's early judicial appointments, "The Kennedy Judicial Appointments."

are transmitted are not necessarily neutral ones which would ensure the application of a rule substantially similar to that enunciated by the Supreme Court.

Separate from the formal judicial structure but occupying a strategic position as message-transmitter are the states' attorneys general, the chief legal officers of the states. It is customary for attorneys general, when requested, to handle legal questions of interpretation and application of Supreme Court rulings. The opinions rendered are advisory only, but they are generally followed as controlling until a court of law holds otherwise. In quantitative terms, these officials play a more significant transmission role than does the court system. What has been noted concerning the district judge and his local orientation and its effect on his role as transmitter can also be cited with respect to the attorneys general. Krislov has found these individuals likewise to be locally oriented and quite inclined to follow the maxim of "vox populi vox Dei," [9] and a review of their treatment of the Court's rulings on religious exercises in the public schools shows a consequent lack of uniformity.[10] In the state of Illinois, however, it has been the practice of the attorney general to relay queries pertaining to religious practices in the public schools to the State Superintendent of Public Instruction. This channel of transmission is of particular relevance to the study at hand.

• *The Superintendent of Public Instruction as Transmitter*

The Illinois Superintendent of Public Instruction is a constitutional office; incumbents of the position are authorized to render legal opinions in their area of jurisdiction on the same basis as the state's attorney general. Most legal questions involving school affairs come directly to the superintendent, or, if originally directed to the attorney general, they are forwarded to his office. The superintendent is seldom a lawyer, but he has his "legal advisor," who is the *de facto* legal voice of the state educational apparatus.

The legal advisor operates much like an attorney general. The

9. Samuel Krislov, "Constituency versus Constitutionalism: The Desegregation Issue and Tensions and Aspirations of Southern Attorneys General," 3 *Midwest Journal of Political Science* 75 (1959).

10. For a summary of opinions regarding religion in public schools see *Digest and Analysis of State Attorney General Opinions Relating to Freedom of Religion and Separation of Church and State,* prepared by the Commission on Law and Social Action of the American Jewish Congress (New York, 1959).

advisor, hence the superintendent, renders an opinion only in response to a query. Thus he does not, on his own initiative, interpret a ruling of the U.S. Supreme Court. These opinions of his are public, but in a very limited sense. They are public to the degree that those who made the query receive the opinion, as does anyone who may go to the advisor's Springfield office and request to see the opinions which have been rendered.

The office also has printed a booklet entitled "Supreme Court Decisions Concerning Reading of the Bible and Religious Education in the Public Schools," [11] which uniformly accompanies an opinion of the superintendent. This booklet contains the full reports of the *McCollum, Zorach,* and *Engel* decisions as well as an important Illinois decision, *People ex rel. Jeremiah Ring v. Board of Education,*[12] and a summary statement of the Court's position on religious education in the schools. This summary ends with the statement:

> It is the opinion of this office that all school districts which are co-operating with groups promoting religious education in such manner as to come into conflict with principles announced above, should cause such activities to be discontinued or changed to comply with these views. Any new programs contemplated should certainly be in accord with the principles announced by the Court. The schools of Illinois should exhibit the highest example of obedience to and compliance with the laws of our State and Nation.[13]

This authoritative statement of "the law" was not given general distribution to the school districts for guidance. It was merely available on request.

The advisor is often presented with questions for which the Court's "wall of separation" formula gives little direction. For instance, what does this formula have to say about baccalaureate services, Christmas or Thanksgiving programs, the use of religious themes in art classes, or the employment of garbed nuns as teachers? Plainly the advisor is left to his own devices to make the interpretations. On the whole, the advisor took a fairly broad view of the Court's rulings, as the following discussion demonstrates.

11. Circular Series A, No. 150, issued by Ray Page, Superintendent of Public Instruction, Illinois (1950). This apparently descended from the bulletin promulgated by the Superintendent of Public Instruction in the wake of the *McCollum* decision to guide local school officials in complying with the ruling, which had applied very directly to the State of Illinois.

12. 245 Ill. 334 (1910).

13. Circular Series A, No. 150, p. 6.

The advisor's interpretations result partially from the fact that the situation has been structured for him by earlier legal action in Illinois. In the 1910 *Ring* case, mentioned above, the plaintiffs sought the discontinuance of the singing of hymns, the recitation of the Lord's Prayer, and the reading of the Bible as public school exercises. The Illinois Supreme Court agreed with the plaintiffs that such practices constituted religious worship and sectarian instruction in contravention of the Illinois constitution.[14] In addition, the Illinois Constitution as well as the School Code prohibit the use of public funds for church or sectarian purposes.[15] Recent opinions regarding religious practices in public schools have included citation of these rulings. After 1962, of course, the *Engel* and *Schempp* decisions of the U.S. Supreme Court also were cited.[16]

In his responses to queries, the advisor generally noted that there were no court decisions prohibiting the specific practices questioned but the opinions he rendered usually took a quite cautious line.[17] For instance, in response to queries about school assemblies commemorating religious observances, he typically recommended that such programs be held outside school hours or, if held on school time, that they emphasize the festive nature of the observances—the bountiful harvest or the turkey for Thanksgiving, the snow, Santa Claus, or Rudolph for Christmas, a springtime reawakening theme for Easter—rather than celebrate the more obvious religious elements. When asked about the use of Christmas subjects for art work, the advisor's response was:

> It would seem to me that the recommendation that should be made to your art instructors is to limit the Christmas art instruction to scenes of Christmas cheer, the festive spirit, the wintry aspects of Christmas, but do not involve the children in the more deeply religious elements of the season.[18]

14. 245 Ill. 334 (1910).

15. Illinois Constitution, Article VII, Sec. 1; Illinois School Code, *Illinois Revised Statutes,* Ch. 122, sec. 22-10, p. 1984.

16. The legal advisor's entire file of correspondence related to religious exercises in public schools for the three-year period 1962–64 was examined. This is the relevant period, as it begins prior to the *Engel* ruling and encompasses the *Schempp* decision.

17. Opinion of September 21, 1963, to Roy C. Hawley, Superintendent of LaSalle County Schools, regarding Christmas programs: "Inasmuch as this is a very precarious subject on which our State courts have never ruled, it must be handled very carefully by each local school administrator and school board in order that there will be no violation of the Constitutional privileges guaranteed all children."

18. Opinion of November 26, 1962, to R. B. Mades, Superintendent of Kane County Schools.

The advisor does not limit himself to responses to the inquiries of school administrators but also responds to all requests for information and opinion from interested persons. These responses may become eventually important variables in the resolution of related conflicts at the local level. For example, a member of the board of directors of a rural school district in southern Illinois wrote of the periodic visits to the school classrooms by an evangelist and his wife for the teaching of Bible verses and the telling of Bible stories "of their own interpretation." [19] As a school director, this individual protested to other board members and the principal, but his protests fell on deaf ears. The advisor found such practices contrary to the Illinois School Code and the Constitution, in his opinion stating that "the procedure you describe is not authorized and the Board should see that it is discontinued immediately." [20]

Private citizens similarly can draw upon the resources of the state office to cope with a local situation. A parent, for example, protested the distribution of religious material in his child's classroom and received this sympathetic response on the part of the advisor:

> In reply I advise that I agree with your contention that any type of religious or spiritual instruction in the tax-supported schools of Illinois is contrary to the Constitution and court decisions on the subject. Therefore, the school board of your district should see to it that the teacher in question is instructed to discontinue handing out religious booklets to the pupils.
>
> For your convenience in referring to court rulings, I am sending you a copy of a bulletin prepared by this office. . . . I am sure that you will find it helpful in convincing the board that the procedure you have described is illegal.[21]

In another instance a private citizen objected to a variety of practices conducted in the public schools in his locale, among them the use of an opening prayer at graduation. In his response the advisor acknowledged the limits of the resources of the Office of Public Instruction but informed the inquirer of the action which could be taken by him:

> I wish to advise you that it is my opinion that this violates the doctrine of separation of church and state, which doctrine has been reiterated just

19. Letter of December 16, 1963, to Superintendent Page from Gene Crawford of Eldorado, Ill.
20. Opinion of December 17, 1963.
21. Opinion of January 2, 1964, to Paul J. Taul, Hettick, Ill.

> recently by the U.S. Supreme Court (*Engel v. Vitale*). Our office has repeatedly informed school boards as to this wall between Church and State and I think that most of them are well informed on the subject. This office, however, does not have the power to enforce the court decision.
>
> As you will have noted from the recent Supreme Court case, it was actually brought by the parents of children attending the school, and that is the way those law suits are instituted.
>
> If you and the other citizens of your group are interested in this problem, the method would be for you to follow the example of those parents in New York and institute a legal proceeding against the school officials to determine by a competent jurisdiction whether or not they are in violation of the separation of church and state.[22]

In short, while the State Superintendent of Public Instruction may not inject himself officially into disputes of this nature at the local level, an opinion from his office at the request of one of the disputants could be an important variable in a local controversy. Individuals seeking a change in local practices and finding themselves unable to effect one could buttress their contention with a sympathetic opinion from the superintendent's office. The substance of these opinions, as the above quotations strongly suggest, were rewarding to those who wish to maintain a very rigid sort of separation between educational instruction and religious practices. While the state office, through the legal advisor, has the difficult task of applying the Court's rulings to instances far removed from those which stimulated the judicial response, it enjoys much the same sort of advantage as the U.S. Supreme Court, which rendered the original rulings—that of distance. The advisor, as a legal "expert" and not a directly involved participant, can afford to give the sort of simplistic, absolutist opinion that a more directly involved local participant would find difficult or impossible to render. However, the participation by the state office is discontinuous, coming only in response to direct appeals and having no general impact or legal validity.

22. Opinion of July 3, 1962, to J. Blecheisen of Roseclare, Ill.

CHAPTER 6

Transmission: Extralegal Channels

THE FORMAL CHANNELS that we have just discussed in Chapter 5 were of little moment to people in Eastville-Westville, since no one used them. These are the only formal channels by which rulings get from the Court down to the level of implementation. Yet information concerning these decisions did get to Eastville-Westville, they were accepted by significant elements of the population, and they were implemented. This suggests, of course, that there are important channels of transmission which are not legally provided for but which nevertheless perform a vital role in the Supreme Court's decision-making system.

The mass media were by far the most important source of information for the people of this district and were the principal source to which they turned for help in forming opinions on these issues.[1] In this chapter we shall survey the treatment given the *Engel* and *Schempp* rulings by the media relevant to Eastville-Westville in order to see what view of them the residents of the district received. Admittedly, little can be said in this necessarily ex post facto analysis about the influence these media had on attitude formation. The *Engel* ruling was handed down nearly two years prior to this study, while the *Schempp* ruling came nearly one year prior. Nevertheless, it is suggested that the accounts of the rulings comprise some incalculable part of the background for the opinions and knowledge of many in the district. Thus we continue our concern with the adequacy of channels of transmission.

1. See Appendix B, items 12 and 13—which involve the ways in which people became aware of the Court's religion-in-public-school decisions—and the respective response frequencies.

• *Newspapers*

The newspaper is the primary means by which the respondents were apprised of the Court's rulings. Thus a careful analysis of local press treatment is in order. Eastville and Westville depend on outside sources for their news of happenings in the greater world. Both villages have their own newspapers, but these are of no importance to us here as they focus entirely on the social life of the two communities. For exposure to the outside world the residents of this locale turn primarily to newspapers from the larger cities in the area—the Decatur *Review* and *Herald,* the Bloomington *Pantagraph,* and the Champaign-Urbana *News-Gazette.*[2] For nonlocal news, these papers are in turn primarily dependent upon the large national news services. The view of national and international happenings conveyed to the people of Eastville and Westville, then, is through the eyes of the Associated Press, United Press International, and the *New York Times* News Service.

»The Newspaper and *Engel v. Vitale*

That the newspaper is an important means for the transmission of Supreme Court policy was given "judicial notice" by an insider, Associate Justice Tom Clark. In an appearance before the Cosmopolitan Club of San Francisco a scant month after the *Engel* ruling, Clark acknowledged that the Court had received a greater outpouring of criticism through telegrams and the mails than at any time in recent history. He felt that much of the public's criticism stemmed from a lack of understanding which was in part attributable to the handling of the ruling by the wire services.[3]

Despite the fact that he seldom commented publicly upon particular rulings—a generally accepted rule of the judicial code—Clark felt compelled to state in very clear terms what the court had actually said in the *Engel* case. He summarized it as follows:

2. The relevant newspapers were not determined by questionnaire responses but were determined on the basis of interviews. One additional newspaper was occasionally cited—the Champaign-Urbana *Courier.* Inasmuch as this was less frequently cited, and since it is published by the Lindsey-Schaub chain, which also publishes the Decatur *Review* and contains the same wire stories as well as editorials, it is not included in the following analysis.

3. William A. Hachten, "Journalism and the Prayer Decision," *Columbia Journalism Review* (Fall, 1962), pp. 4–8.

> . . . here was a state-written prayer circulated to state-employed teachers with instructions to have their pupils recite it in unison at the beginning of each school day. The Constitution says that government shall take no part in the establishment of religion. No means no. As soon as the people learned that this was all the Court said—not that there could be no official recognition of a Divine Being, or recognition on silver or currency of "In God We Trust," or public acknowledgement that we are a religious nation—they understood the basis upon which the Court acted.[4]

Public misunderstanding was attributed in part to "pressures on reporters to communicate the ruling rapidly, with half a dozen other major decisions." [5] The Justice noted that the news releases

> were not complete, most of them reciting the content of the twenty-two word prayer and the fact that the Court had held it unconstitutional for a teacher to have her pupils recite it.[6]

This speech drew the ire of representatives of the wire services, who felt that such criticism was unjustified.[7] Does a study of the treatment accorded *Engel v. Vitale* by the press relevant to Eastville-Westville tend to substantiate Justice Clark's contention? If it does, then the adequacy of newspapers as transmitters of Court messages must be seriously questioned.

The first reports in the newspapers on the evening of the decision were sparse as far as the Court's reasoning was concerned. The *Pantagraph* and the *Review* both carried the Associated Press article which quoted, in seven lines of the article, the portion of Black's opinion which merely announces the result:

> We think that by using its public school system to encourage recitation of the regents' prayer, the state of New York has adopted a practice wholly inconsistent with the establishment clause of the U.S. Constitution.

4. Quoted, *ibid.*, p. 4.

5. *Ibid.* Unfortunately for the Court, one of those other "major decisions" involved the striking down of a Post Office Department order which had banned from the mail a number of lewd magazines allegedly appealing to the prurient interests of homosexuals. For some it was incongruous for the Court to ban school prayers and allow the distribution of homosexual literature all on the same day!

6. *Ibid.* An account of Clark's speech is also contained in "Clark Explains Prayer Decision," San Francisco *Chronicle,* August 4, 1962, p. 1, cols. 6 and 7.

7. "Reporters Disavow Prayer Ruling Haze," *Editor and Publisher,* August 11, 1962, p. 11.

This was followed, in thirteen lines of newspaper text, by excerpts from the dissenting opinion of Justice Stewart, who felt that "the Court has misapplied a great constitutional law principle." The article went on to quote Stewart:

> I cannot see how an "official religion" is established by letting those who want to say a prayer say it. On the contrary, I think that to deny the wish of these school children to join in reciting this prayer is to deny them the opportunity of sharing in the spiritual heritage of our nation.

The *Review* went on to present, in capsule form, the arguments for the opposing sides—material omitted from the *Pantagraph* account.[8] Thus the rationale for Stewart's dissent was presented, while that of the majority opinion was not.

The newspapers of the next day provided fuller accounts and included more of the rationale for the decision. The Decatur *Herald* carried a later Associated Press account which placed the instant decision into the context of "establishment" cases which had come before—*Everson, McCollum,* and *Zorach.* Although the portion of Stewart's dissent included in earlier AP stories was quoted, another selection from Black's majority opinion was excerpted which gets closer to the heart of the majority's reasoning:

> When the power, prestige, and financial support of government is placed behind a particular religious belief, the indirect coercive pressure upon religious minorities to conform to the prevailing officially approved religion is plain.

This dispatch carried the first notices of opposition to the ruling, particularly in the South, where previous Court rulings had also been unpopular.[9]

In the evening papers of the following day, the emphasis in the wire-service articles was on the controversy which had started to boil as a result of the *Engel* ruling. The Champaign-Urbana *News-Gazette,* which had not carried an article the previous day, proclaimed in two-inch banner headlines on page one: "Prayer Decision Stirs Anger," followed by "Greatest Controversy Since Racial Decision." This United Press International (UPI) article led off with a report of

8. "Supreme Court Bans Prayer in New York Public Schools," Decatur *Review,* June 25, 1962, p. 1, col. 8; and Bloomington *Pantagraph,* "Public School Prayer Ruled Unconstitutional," June 25, 1962, p. 1, col. 5.

9. "School Prayer Banned as Violating Constitution," Decatur *Herald,* June 26, p. 1, cols. 6 and 7.

Maryland Senator J. Glenn Beall's intention to offer an offsetting constitutional amendment and related that the "reaction of religious leaders ranged from approbation to shock and dismay." After dealing with such reactions to the decision, the account dwelt on the majority opinion, quoting from Black that

> government in this country, be it state or federal, is without power to prescribe by law any particular form of prayer which is to be used as an official prayer in carrying on any program or governmentally sponsored religious activity.

The Stewart dissent was likewise noted, but this time the story emphasized the dissenter's point that a great many religious practices are traditional parts of government activity, such as the opening of Congressional sessions with a prayer and the Court's own crier opening its sessions with "God save the United States and this honorable Court." [10]

Subsequent articles appearing on the news pages (we shall deal with editorial reaction later) were uniformly concerned with public reaction to the decision, particularly on the part of churchmen and political leaders. The response in Congress—where two days of vitriolic debate followed the decision and forty-two proposals for offsetting constitutional amendments were introduced—produced a number of related articles in the two weeks following the decision. Only three stories of local origin appeared on the news pages; one dealt with reactions by local school and religious leaders in Champaign-Urbana,[11] and identical articles in each of the Decatur papers commented on the effect of the ruling in its schools.[12]

The individual newspaper is not powerless in its treatment of the news on its pages. Certainly it is free to print its own articles, as did three of these papers, and to comment on events of its choosing on its editorial pages. Beyond this, the local newspaper plays an important role in that its staff is responsible for the manner in which nationally originated news articles are presented to its readers. It is the local staff that positions these articles on the page, determines the pages on which the articles will be placed, and chooses the wording of the

10. Louis Cassels, "Prayer Decision Stirs Anger," Champaign-Urbana *News-Gazette,* June 26, p. 1, cols. 7 and 8.

11. Sandy Schurter, "Local Religious Leaders Deplore Prayer Ban," Champaign-Urbana *News-Gazette,* June 26, p. 3, col. 1.

12. "Prayers Not in Decatur Public Schools," Decatur *Herald,* June 26, p. 1, col. 6; and Decatur *Review,* June 26, p. 3, col. 6.

headlines. These are important variables in determining how the reader will react to the news.[13]

While the body of a news story may be the most significant factor in helping to shape opinion, the headline is, in Schramm's terms, an "indexing cue," which calls the prospective reader's attention to the nature of the signs embodied in the article. Schramm suggests that the reader selects the cues which "seem to have the greatest predictive value . . . which seem to promise him the greatest reward." [14] Not only does the headline draw the reader's attention, but Tannenbaum's research suggests also that it

> establishes the frame of reference within which the facts of the story are perceived. It creates the first mood or impression which subtly and perhaps unconsciously dominates the reader's attention as he peruses the whole story. In a way, it provides a lens through which the remainder of the story or article is perceived.[15]

The newspaper headline, then, may be profitably investigated to ascertain the impression of the ruling as generated in the newspapers. The importance of this aspect is underscored by the fact that a majority of readers do little but skim the newspaper and read the headlines.[16]

Table 2 lists in chronological order the headlines of relevant articles published in the four sample newspapers for a two-week period following the *Engel* ruling. As to be expected, a great flurry of articles was published on the two days immediately following the decision, while the output markedly tapered off toward the end of the period. The headlines, as do their accompanying articles, fall into two general classes: (1) those dealing with the announcement of the decision itself and (2) those concerned with reaction to the decision.

13. Charles E. Swanson, "What They Read in 130 Daily Newspapers," 32 *Journalism Quarterly* 411 (1955); Wilbur Schramm, "The Nature of News," 26 *Journalism Quarterly* 259 (1949); and Percy H. Tannenbaum, "The Effects of Headlines on the Interpretation of News Stories," 30 *Journalism Quarterly* 189 (1953).

14. Schramm, *op. cit.*, p. 267. Schramm, drawing from Freud, suggests that there are two types of rewards involved: (1) immediate reward, where the reader can enjoy a vicarious experience such as reading about accidents, crime, corruption, social events, or other elements without immediate reality; and (2) delayed reward, where the immediate value lies in being informed and prepared, with the payoff in possible later rewards.

15. Tannenbaum, *op. cit.*, p. 197.

16. Survey Research Center, "Interest, Information and Attitudes in the Field of World Affairs" (November, 1949), cited in V. O. Key, Jr., *Public Opinion and American Democracy* (New York: Alfred A. Knopf, 1961), pp. 352 f. Key notes that "day in and day out the odds are that less than 10% of the adult population could be regarded as careful readers of the political news" (p. 353).

Table 2

Newspaper Article Headlines on *Engel v. Vitale*

1963 Date	Headline	Newspaper [a]	Article Source [b]	Page
6–25	"Public School Prayer Ruled Unconstitutional"	P	AP	1
6–25	"Supreme Court Bans Prayer in New York Public Schools"	R	AP	1
6–26	"School Prayer Banned as Violating Constitution"	H	AP	1
6–26	"Prayers Not in Decatur Public School Routine"	H	L	1
6–26	"Prayer Decision Stirs Anger"	N-G	UPI	1
6–26	"Local Religious Leaders Deplore Prayer Ban"	N-G	L	3
6–26	"No Conflict in State on Prayer Ban"	N-G	UPI	3
6–26	"Prayer Ruling Stirs Caldron of Criticism"	P	AP	1
6–26	"Churchmen Hit Ban of Prayer"	R	AP	1
6–27	"Congressmen Would Change Constitution Allow Prayers"	H	AP	1
6–27	"Lawmakers Seethe over Prayer Ban"	R	AP	35
6–27	"Overriding Court Viewed as Doubtful"	P	AP	1
6–27	"Doubt is Cast on Prayer Bill"	N-G	AP	1
6–28	"Kennedy: Pray at Home"	H	AP	1
6–28	"Support Prayer Ruling—Kennedy"	P	AP	1
7–1	"Prayer Ban Backed by Methodist Group"	N-G	UPI	3
7–1	"Court Ruled Against God: Goldwater"	N-G	UPI	6
7–2	"Ministers Speak Out on Decision"	N-G	AP	1
7–2	"Governors Plan School Prayer Appeal"	H	N.Y.T.	1
7–2	"Analyst Probes Meaning of Court's Prayer Ruling"	N-G	AP	1
7–2	"Pastors Split on Prayer Ban"	R	AP	1
7–3	"Governors Back School Prayers"	H	N.Y.T.	1
7–5	"Arends Disagrees on Prayer Ruling"	N-G	L	13

[a] P = Bloomington *Pantagraph;* H = Decatur *Herald;* R = Decatur *Review;* N-G = Champaign-Urbana *News-Gazette*.

[b] AP = Associated Press; N.Y.T. = *New York Times* News Service; UPI = United Press International; L = local article.

The headlines which announced the result are correct as far as they go, but they are obviously too brief to convey the full meaning of the ruling. In no instance does a headline of this category indicate that the banned prayer was one composed by state officials and prescribed by a school board—both relevant considerations as far as the Court was concerned. Nor do these headlines convey the idea that only this sort of prayer was banned by this specific decision. These criticisms do not apply simply to the four papers comprising our sample, for the same kinds of headlines appeared throughout the nation. Inaccurate headlines were considered partially responsible for the great confusion surrounding the decision.[17] While an editor cannot capture all the subtleties of a complex decision in a headline, it is unfortunate that, for many readers, their knowledge and impression of a decision depends solely upon these few short words.

Viewing headlines of the second category—those concerned with reaction to the decision—we see in very vivid terms that the decision drew sharp criticism. Anger was stirred up; there was an actual "caldron of criticism." Prestigious individuals were greatly distressed by the ruling; religious leaders were said to "deplore" the decision and were attempting to find ways to upset it. One influential senator, in fact, opined that the "Court ruled against God." In the period studied, only a few headlines indicated any degree of support for the ruling.

The articles which followed these headlines were relatively accurate accounts. In dealing with reaction to the decision, an effort was uniformly made to present views from both sides of the controversy. If there is a fault here, it would lie in the fact that opposing reactions were generally allocated a greater amount of space than supporting statements. However, the opponents of the decision were much more vocal at this time than the supporters. Regardless of how well the articles were balanced, Table 2 makes it strikingly clear that newspaper readers in the Eastville-Westville School District were told through their newspaper headlines that the Court had ruled prayer in school unconstitutional and that political and religious leaders in general were distressed with the decision and were seeking ways to counter its effects.

A somewhat different view of the *Engel* decision emerges from the editorial pages of our sample. Viewing the headlines, which once again "index" the sets of stimuli embodied in the text of the editorial, we see

17. Hachten, *op. cit.*, p. 5.

from Table 3 that they are, with few exceptions, more restrained and less spectacular than those found heading articles on the news pages. In addition, they were found to be quite indicative of the substance of the article. This difference may reflect the dissimilarity between the audience of the editorial page and that of the news pages. Those who look at the editorial page at all are likely to read a good portion of the articles and are not as influenced by layout characteristics as the general newspaper reader.[18]

The editorial pages were also found to give a much more balanced and complete treatment to the topics selected for discussion. Table 3 indicates that articles concerning the decision did not appear on the editorial pages until two days after the decision. The writers were able to develop their ideas and were not under the deadline pressure of those who write page-one copy. Roscoe Drummond put it quite succinctly when he admitted sharing in "the first flush of emotional distaste for the Court's ruling," but contemplation had convinced him that there was "no good alternative to accepting [the decision] in good spirit and good faith." [19] A good number of the columns were able to dwell upon what the Court did not say—upon the limits of the decision. The editorial in the *Pantagraph* was of this nature, as were the syndicated columns of Lawrence and Edson in particular. In fact, David Lawrence quoted the footnote by Black in the majority decision, which, had it been given wider distribution, would possibly have quelled much of the antagonism toward the decision, since it specified that the Court's ruling did not touch many other references to the Deity which are manifest in public life.[20]

The editorial comment, of course, was not all favorably disposed toward the ruling, especially with respect to the newspaper's own position. Only the *Pantagraph* [21] did not take a negative stand, and the *News-Gazette* did not commit itself editorially at all. The Decatur papers were both in oppositon. The *Herald,* in its June 27th editorial, was primarily concerned with the implications of the *Engel* decision for the many other observances by which the nation's religious heritage is recognized; this was an apparent major source of concern for many

18. Dean C. Baker and James C. MacDonald, "Newspaper Editorial Readership and Length of Editorials," 38 *Journalism Quarterly* 473 (1961).

19. "Ruling Should Be Supported," Decatur *Review,* July 3, 1962, p. 4, cols. 4–7.

20. "Court Bars Only 'Official' Prayers," *Pantagraph,* June 28, 1962, p. 4. For text of this footnote see Chapter 4, p. 51.

21. To avoid citing each of the articles mentioned, other than those quoted, attention is directed to Table 3 for the relevant information.

TABLE 3

Editorial-Page Comment in Four Newspapers on *Engel v. Vitale*

1963 Date	Headline	Newspaper [a]	Article Source [b]	Editorial Tenor [c]
6–27	"Extend Thesis of Court Ruling on School Prayer?"	H	Ed.	–
6–27	"A Dissent—The Court Was Right"	H	Ed.	+
6–27	"David Felts' Column"	H	D. Felts	–
6–27	"Supreme Court's Ruling on School Prayer"	R	Ed.	–
6–28	"Let Reason Prevail on Prayer Ruling"	P	Ed.	0
6–28	"Court Bars Only 'Official Prayers' "	P	D. Lawrence	0
6–28	"Prayer Not Barred By Court Rule"	N-G	D. Lawrence	0
6–29	"Court Decision in Prayer Adds to General Confusion"	H	A. Lewis	–
6–29	"Court Flips in Prayer Ruling"	R	A. Krock	–
7–1	" 'Aid to Religion' Hit by Douglas"	N-G	D. Lawrence	0
7–1	"The Nature of Prayer"	H, R	Ed.	–
7–2	"Historic Meeting Led to Court's Prayer Decision"	N-G	D. Pearson	+
7–3	"Supreme Court Opinion in Decision Against School Prayer"	R	Ed.	0
7–3	"Americans Are Religious People"	N-G	G. Sokolsky	–
7–3	"Prayer Ruling Not Blow at Religion"	P	P. Edson	+
7–3	"Ruling Should Be Supported"	R	R. Drummond	+
7–4	"National Anthem as Prayer"	H, R	Ed.	–
7–5	"Why Does Court Deny God?"	N-G	G. Sokolsky	–
7–5	"Morality Can Be Taught in Schools"	N-G	D. Lawrence	0
7–6	"Ruling Will Not Heathenize"	H	R. McGill	+

[a] H = Decatur *Herald;* R = Decatur *Review;* N-G = Champaign-Urbana *News-Gazette;* P = Bloomington *Pantagraph.*

[b] Names are those of syndicated columnists, while "Ed." notes an unsigned editorial expressing the paper's position, or article placed by editor.

[c] A plus sign (+) indicates an editorial supporting the decision, while a minus sign (–) indicates opposition. A zero (0) indicates neutrality—where the author states no opinion but discusses the decision or its implications.

people. Anthony Lewis, of the *New York Times,* perhaps the most astute of the journalists covering the Court at the time, was perplexed about this as well, saying that it was "impossible to determine what the Supreme Court will or will not allow" and citing inconsistencies in the Court's previous treatment of the issue.[22] Lewis' colleague on the *Times,* Arthur Krock, made somewhat the same point but in a more vitriolic article, which appeared in the Decatur *Review*. Interestingly, the Decatur *Herald* contained a dissenting editorial from a member of the staff who disagreed with the majority of his colleagues, this article being carried on the same day as the paper's "majority" editorial opinion. The *Review* also editorialized against the *Engel* ruling on the grounds that the Court displayed rather strained reasoning in extending the prohibition against religious establishment to the Regents' public school prayer.

While there were a number of negative articles appearing on the editorial pages, there were in each of the four newspapers others specifically favorable or at least neutral in their presentation. The *Review,* for example, even carried extended portions of the majority opinion by Black and also excerpts from Stewart's dissent. While the neutral articles of this kind took no specific stand in favor of or against the ruling, they could be classified as aiding their readers in understanding what the Court had said, thus performing a positive function. The articles specifically opposing the ruling were, for the most part, calm and reasoned in their opposition. Exceptions to this were the two columns by George Sokolsky appearing in the *News-Gazette,* which were, as the headlines reproduced in Table 3 indicate, inflammatory, to say the least, and constituted the only direct attack on the Court itself.[23]

Readers who exposed themselves to the editorial pages at this time had the opportunity to read articles which gave a full treatment to the decision and to read both sides of the question in each of the four newspapers. By the same token, however, since the four newspapers

22. "Court Decision in Prayer Adds to General Confusion," Decatur *Herald,* June 29, 1962, p. 10, col. 7.

23. Sokolsky noted that most of the judges do not list religious affiliation in *Who's Who* and stated that these "black-robed" secularists could not "erase God from our hearts . . ." ("Americans Are Religious People," *News-Gazette,* July 3, 1962, p. 8, col. 7). He later saw the decision as encouraging atheism and agnosticism and advocated silent prayer in the schools, with the children adding to their prayers the words: "And may God bless the United States Supreme Court with Sanity" ("Why Does Court Deny God?" *News-Gazette,* July 5, 1962, p. 8, col. 7).

carried columns both favorable and unfavorable to the ruling on their editorial pages, the reader was presented with an opportunity to choose to read those articles which reinforced the commitment which he brought with him to the editorial pages.[24]

Review of the treatment accorded *Engel v. Vitale* by the newspapers read in Eastville-Westville suggests that Justice Clark's criticism of the press was somewhat justified. As far as the general reader was concerned, a rather negative impression was generated through the headlines and the terse news articles. However, well-balanced and reasoned coverage was available to those who chose to read the editorial pages. It can be said in defense of the press, on the other hand, that the Court itself tended to obscure and leave unanswered certain problems found to be most perplexing to the public. It is possible to suggest that the Court learned its lesson in this regard, for its decision in the *Schempp* case avoided certain of these pitfalls.

»Newspapers and the *Schempp* Ruling

The formal hearings of the *Schempp* and *Murray* cases were held on February 27, 1963, and the wire services carried reports of restrained but open antagonism in court between Justices Black and Stewart over the relationship between the establishment clause and the free-exercise clause.[25] On its last opinion day of the session the Court's announced decision again reached the public through page-one stories in the press.

Newspaper readers in the Eastville-Westville district were apprised of the Court's determination on the very afternoon of the decision. Of the three afternoon papers, two—the *Pantagraph* and the *Review*—carried the Associated Press account, which stressed, from Clark's majority opinion, the notion that strict neutrality on the part of the government must be maintained and that not even minor encroachments could be tolerated. Singled out for attention and specific quotation were those portions of the decision that set limits to the present decision in that they stated that objective study of the Bible is not inconsistent with the First Amendment and that the

> place of religion in our society is an exalted one, achieved through a long tradition of reliance on the home, the church and the inviolable

24. This sort of phenomenon was mentioned in Paul Lazarsfeld, Bernard Berelson, and Hazel Gaudet, *The People's Choice* (New York: Duell, Sloan & Pearce, 1945), p. 124.

25. United Press International, "School Prayer Issue Starts Court Fight," Springfield *Illinois State Register*, February 27, 1963, p. 1, col. 1.

> citadel of the individual heart and mind. We have come to recognize through bitter experience that it is not within the power of government to invade that citadel, whether its purpose or effect be to aid or oppose, to advance or retard. In the relationship between man and religion, the State is firmly committed to a position of neutrality.

Extensive quotes from Stewart's dissent, particularly his argument that additional evidence of coercion was necessary, completed the article.[26]

The *News-Gazette* carried a much shorter United Press International version on page one but relegated it to the bottom of the page in columns five and six. The article, without quotation, noted that the Court ruled "that use of the Lord's Prayer and Bible reading as devotional opening exercises in public schools is unconstitutional," citing the First and Fourteenth Amendments. It then gave a brief account of the two programs upset by the ruling.[27]

The following day, the morning Decatur *Herald* carried a *New York Times* News Service account which, while featuring the excerpts from Clark's opinion, quoted above, labeled the decision "a final legal answer to one of the most divisive issues of church and state." "The Justices," the article noted, "were evidently concerned to prevent, as best they could, the bitter criticism that greeted the New York Case." It went on to indicate that

> Justice Clark stressed the importance of religion in the country's tradition. He took care to say that the decision did not affect the right to use the Bible for teaching purposes or deal with such other matters as army chaplains.[28]

The news services, then, were quick to pick up the portion of Clark's dicta which explicitly stated the limits of the ruling and which acknowledged the traditional place of religion in American society. In the *Engel* decision the Court had neglected this explicit recognition, except for the footnote by Justice Black. This footnote, as we have seen, was not picked up on the news pages—a fact which perhaps contributed to the storm of criticism which greeted the *Engel* decision.

Press response to the *Schempp* decision is presented in Table 4. Concentrating on the two weeks immediately following the decision,

26. "High Court Rules Required Bible Reading, Lord's Prayer in Schools Unconstitutional," Decatur *Daily Review,* June 17, 1963, p. 1, col. 5.

27. "Court Reaffirms Prayer Ruling," Champaign-Urbana *News-Gazette,* June 17, 1963, p. 1, cols. 5 and 6.

28. "Court Bars School Required Bible Reading, Lord's Prayer," Decatur *Herald,* June 18, 1963.

Table 4

Newspaper Article Headlines on *Abington Township School District v. Schempp*

1963 Date	Headline	Newspaper[a]	Article Source[a]	Page
6–17	"High Court Bans School Devotions"	P	AP	1
6–17	"Court Reaffirms Prayer Ruling"	N-G	UPI	1
6–17	"High Court Rules Required Bible Reading and Lord's Prayer Unconstitutional in Schools"	R	AP	1
6–18	"Court Bars School Required Bible Reading, Lord's Prayer"	H	N.Y.T.	1
6–18	"Rule on School Devotions Encourages Objective Study"	P	UPI	1
6–18	"Move to Reverse Prayer Ruling Appears Doomed"	N-G	UPI	1
6–18	"Clergy, Laymen Reaction Mixed"	N-G	UPI	1
6–18	"Clergy Reaction Differs on Ban of School Prayer"	N-G	Staff	3
6–18	"Church Reaction to Court Decision Mostly Favorable"	H	N.Y.T.	8
6–18	"Congressional Court Critics Less Angry"	H	AP	8
6–18	"Court Decision Draws Mild Reaction"	R	AP	1
6–19	"Constitution Should Permit Bible: Cushing"	H	AP	5
6–19	"Religious Freedom Protected by the Court"	P	Ed.	4
6–19	"Decision by Supreme Court Separates Education, Religion"	P	D. Lawrence	4
6–19	"Establishment Not the Issue"	H	Ed.	8
6–19	"Prayer in Public Schools"	R	Ed.	8
6–19	"Jefferson Sustained"	R	A. Krock	8
6–20	"Southerners Seek Prayer Amendments"	P	UPI	1
6–21	"Court Clarifies Religious Rule"	N-G	D. Lawrence	4
6–23	"Politics Grasps a Prayer"	P	Ed.	4
6–23	"Prayer Ruling Draws Mixture of Reactions"	P	UPI	30
6–24	"School Prayer Proponents Grasping at Straw—Lippmann"	P	W. Lippmann	6
6–25	"Rules School Prayers Legal"	P	AP	1
6–25	"How to Explain Court Ruling"	N-G	D. Lawrence	4
6–27	"Rulings Against School Prayers Pleases Only Militant Atheists"	P	R. Kirk	4

[a] See page 77 for symbol listing.

we see a qualitative difference between these headlines and those of the year before. Again much of the copy was concerned with reaction to the decision, but whereas in 1962 the *Engel* ruling had stirred a "caldron of criticism," churchmen "deplored" the decision, and congressmen were "seething," the 1963 decision invoked "less angry" responses from Congress, a "mixed reaction" from the clergy (but "mostly favorable") and in general a "mild reaction." The headline-writers could have seized upon the negative statements of some Southern members of Congress or those of the Reverend Billy Graham or the Bishops Cushing and Spellman, but they did not do so. Qualitatively the headlines were much more restrained; quantitatively the related articles were fewer—fifteen in the two-week 1963 period as opposed to twenty-two in 1962.

The change in tenor was perhaps even more pronounced on the editorial pages. In 1962 all the newspapers which took an editorial position opposed the *Engel* ruling, while in 1963 the same newspapers (again the *News-Gazette* did not editorially comment) favored the *Schempp* decision. The *Pantagraph* was lavish in its praise of the decision, suggesting that "religious leaders . . . should take courage from this decision rather than decry it" and concluding that those who "cherish freedom, and especially freedom of religion, should applaud the decision."[29] The *Herald* also saw the Court aiding religious groups but suggested that there would have been less confusion had the case been argued and determined on the basis of the due-process clause of the Fourteenth Amendment, rather than the establishment clause of the First.[30]

This same change can also be noted on the part of the syndicated columnists. Although they wrote far fewer articles on *Schempp,* only one—the conservative Russell Kirk—wrote in opposition to the ruling, while four of twelve had been decidedly negative toward the *Engel* ruling. The trend toward a more favorable view of the Court's treatment of the religion-in-schools issue, which characterized the news pages, was thus also manifest on the editorial pages, as Table 5 shows.

In this section we have tried to show how the Supreme Court's

29. "Religious Freedom Protected by Court," Bloomington *Pantagraph,* June 19, 1963, p. 4, col. 1.

30. "Establishment Not the Issue," Decatur *Herald,* June 19, 1963, p. 8, col. 1. There is some apparent confusion on the part of the editor, as the establishment clause as applied to the states through the Fourteenth Amendment is the basis for the ruling. He apparently is feeling that the argument should have been via the "free exercise" route.

messages in the *Engel* and *Schempp* cases were seen by the people of the Eastville-Westville district through the most widely read newspapers, since this is the medium, as we have said, through which the residents were chiefly apprised of these decisions. It has been shown that the press gave much more sympathetic treatment to the later decision. The Court, by making the limits of its decision quite explicit in the *Schempp* opinion, perhaps helped create a much better climate for acceptance of its decision than it experienced after the *Engel* ruling. There the decision was quite sweeping, and an important qualifier, which, had it been given wider distribution, might have

TABLE 5

Comparison of Editorial Reaction [a] to *Engel v. Vitale* and *Abington Twp. School District v. Schempp*

	Number of Articles			
	Favorable	Neutral	Negative	Total
Engel	5	6	9	20
Schempp	5	4	1	10

[a] Includes both unsigned editorials and syndicated columns.

quelled some of the disturbance, was relegated to a footnote. Moreover, the press, in its rush to proclaim the tidings, expanded the *Engel* decision well beyond its bounds by not elaborating upon the Court's reasoning, though this elaboration later appeared on the editorial pages. The rulings appear to have benefited from a period of reflection on the part of the writers, for we saw, particularly in the *Engel* case, a much more calm view of the decision on the editorial pages than that displayed on the news pages. Such reflection came too late, perhaps, since reaction to the early stories fueled the fires for later reaction stories. All this may have generated a widespread disposition toward nonacceptance and controversy over the decision.

It is tempting to suggest a significant relationship between the characteristics of the Court's message, the way it was treated in the newspapers, and popular acceptance. The Court, through Justice Clark, took pains to explicate the boundaries of the *Schempp* ruling and to "reassure" the public that religion in America was not in jeopardy. These assurances were transmitted by the press, and the decision seemed to be received with general calm, even though the ruling was even broader in effect than that of *Engel*. However, there are competing hypotheses. First, the result in *Schempp* was expected, following, as it did, close on the heels of the *Engel* ruling; and it was obviously in accord with the dominant thought in the liberal Warren Court.

Second, it may be suggested that the year intervening between the two decisions had possibly brought wider acceptance of or resignation to the Court's reasoning. As was noted in Chapter 2, once a decision has been made, there is often attitude change in the direction of the decision. Newspaper and popular reaction—a more positive and less hostile reaction—may be due more to a gradual acceptance of the Court's position during the 1962–63 period than to any factor having to do with message characteristics.[31]

Finally, it is to be noted that the Midwest is not characterized to as great an extent by religious devotions in the public school as are the South and East.[32] Consequently, the newspaper reaction observed in Eastville-Westville could have been less hostile because the issue was not of great salience. Had newspaper reaction been sampled elsewhere, a different view might have been obtained. But the *Schempp* ruling was given more sympathetic treatment generally by the national news services and seemed to be greeted with wider acceptance throughout the nation.

• *Radio and Television*

The people of Eastville-Westville were exposed to news of the Court's rulings through the electronic media to an extent second only to the daily newspaper.

Qualitatively there was little difference between the treatment given the *Engel* ruling by TV and radio and that which appeared on the news pages. The early accounts which came over the air minutes after the Court had handed down its decision were understandably terse and conformed to the description of them by Justice Clark (see above, p. 70). For instance, the ABC radio network on its 12:55 P.M. newscast re-

31. Involved here, it is suggested, is the same sort of mechanism that V. O. Key notes in regard to the acceptability of election results. That is, voters have generally "made their peace with the situation" after the opposing candidate has won by minimizing the importance of the result (Key, *op. cit.*, p. 479). This is all part of the general adjustment explained by theories of "cognitive consistency," discussed in Chapter 2 and to be further considered in Chapter 9.

32. Richard B. Dierenfield, *Religion in American Public Schools* (Washington, D.C.: Public Affairs Press, 1962), Chap. IV.

ported that "the Court ruled today that the offering of a twenty-two word prayer prescribed by New York State in its public schools violates the United States Constitution." Its subsequent newscasts expanded on this by presenting portions of the Court's reasoning. The other networks treated the news in much the same way. However, the 5:06 P.M. NBC report, while presenting a portion of the Court's rationale, expanded the decision somewhat beyond its rather narrow limits:

> The high tribunal ruled out—as unconstitutional—all public school prayers. The 6-to-1 decision—delivered by Justice Black—said this: "It is no part of the business of government to compose official prayers for any group of American people. . . ." [33]

Thus the radio and TV newscasts, with their characteristic incisiveness and drive to report events "as they happen," conveyed an image of a much broader ruling than was actually handed down. In this regard their treatment was similar to the early news stories. Both media operate under much the same sort of pressures. Similarity in treatment may also be traced to the fact that the networks and the stations rely on the same wire services for much of their news.

Television, however, frequently stands back and gives extensive treatment to current issues. CBS News singled out the Court's religion-in-schools rulings for a series entitled "Storm over the Supreme Court," which was presented in three parts—two after *Engel* and one immediately after the *Schempp* ruling.[34] Some respondents in Eastville-Westville reported seeing these prime-time programs, although we were unable to determine the full extent of the coverage in the community.

The first segment of this series, produced by the respected Fred W. Friendly, was aired on February 20, 1963, exactly one week before the oral arguments in the *Schempp* and *Murray* cases. That this series was a quality production is attested by its *dramatis personae*. The reporter was the well-known Eric Sevareid, while four Americans, distinguished in the fields of arts and letters, read from the opinions of the justices and other related materials: Carl Sandburg, Mark Van Doren, Fredric March, and Archibald MacLeish. For constitutional-law expertise,

33. For this and other examples of radio news coverage of the *Engel* decision see "The Prayer Decision: Network's First Stories," *Columbia Journalism Review* (Winter, 1963), p. 54.

34. These programs were presented between 6:30 and 7:30 P.M., local time, on three Wednesdays—February 20, March 13, and June 19, 1963. Appreciation is extended to CBS News for supplying copies of the scripts.

Sevareid turned to Professor Paul Freund of the Harvard Law School. On the subsequent programs, in addition to Freund, Sevareid called upon law-school deans Rostow (Yale), Griswold (Harvard), Fordham (Pennsylvania), and Forrester (Tulane) for their reactions to the Court's *Engel* and *Schempp* decisions.

The first segment did not deal specifically with the *Engel* decision or with the religion-in-schools issue. It was, rather, a constitutional history, tracing the development of the Court through a number of landmark cases. Emphasized in this development were, as the title suggests, the storms the Court has encountered over the years: the Jeffersonian and Jacksonian clashes with Marshall, the Dred Scott episode, the Franklin Roosevelt court-packing incident, and finally the school-desegregation issue. It was pointed out that a clash of opinion has also been manifested within the Court itself, as shown by the processes of dissent. Singled out for particular emphasis was the widely known difference in philosophy between Hugo Black and Felix Frankfurter. It is interesting to note that Freund went to great lengths to emphasize that the difference was one of basic political philosophy and that, true to the judicial code, there was the utmost mutual respect between the two old antagonists.

Having presented an account of how the Court had, over the years, weathered a variety of storms, the second segment, aired three weeks later, focused on the most recent of the storms—that involving *Engel v. Vitale,* the Regents' Prayer case. This program was, in Sevareid's terms, "a biography of a single decision." [35] On June 19, 1963, the third segment was televised; this dealt with the *Schempp* decision and came only two days after the Court's decision. These programs, as Sevareid suggested, traced the cases from the events with which they were concerned through the trial-preparation and lower-court stages to the Court's decisions and the reactions thereto. The actual litigants and their lawyers described the developments and the reasoning behind their actions.

The passages of each opinion selected for quotation were those which had been emphasized in the press, as we noted in our earlier discussion.[36] They dealt with the idea that striking down the exercises

35. CBS Reports, "Storm over the Supreme Court," Part II (New York: CBS Television Network, 1963), p. 2.

36. For instance: "It is neither sacrilegious nor antireligious to say that each separate government in this country should stay out of the business of writing or sanctioning official prayers and leave that purely religious function to the people themselves and to those the people choose to look to for popular guidance" (*Engel*

did not show a hostility toward religion but that the concept of separation of church and state strengthened both. In responding to a question concerning the confusion over the *Engel* decision's impact on a variety of other church-related public exercises, Freund called attention to the Black footnote as an answer to such confusion.[37] In the last program he noted that "one doesn't have to read the fine print," since Black's qualifier had now been elevated to the text of Clark's majority *Schempp* opinion.[38] Thus the notion that the Court's ruling was not a blow to religion—which seemed to be the dominant fear, particularly after the *Engel* ruling—was given high priority in each of these telecasts.

In sum, this series gave the viewer an opportunity to observe the dynamics of the judicial process. Not only was he informed in depth about the lawsuits—as to their genesis, resolution, and the steps between—but he was also actually instructed on some rather complex legal problems: the basic significance of certiorari determinations, dissenting opinions, and questions of legal and political philosophy in general. Of most immediate import, the Courts rulings on the religion-in-schools issue were placed in broad perspective; two hours were devoted to presenting what the Court had said, to the reasoning of the litigants, and to interpretations by prestigious legal scholars.

• *Magazines*

So far we have dealt with media which reach great numbers of people. Magazines do not reach the masses but are quite important for reaching and influencing specialized audiences. Lazarsfeld and his associates found in their Erie County study that only 15–20 per cent of his respondents were magazine-readers, but these were in the main "politically active and alert people in each social group who were likely to influence the decisions of their fellow citizens—the opinion leaders." [39]

The strength of the magazines lies in the fact that they are not as

---

v. Vitale, 370 U.S. at 435); and: "The place of religion in our society is an exalted one, achieved through a long tradition of reliance on the home, the church and the inviolable citadel of the individual heart and mind. . . . In the relationship between man and religion, the State is firmly committed to a position of neutrality" (*Abington Twp. School District v. Schempp,* 374 U.S. at 226).

37. CBS Reports, Part II, p. 21.

38. *Ibid.,* Part III, pp. 23, 24.

39. Lazarsfeld *et al., op. cit.,* p. 134.

tied to a broad coverage of current events and are thus able to concentrate on fewer issues and to take time to elaborate various points.[40] Because opinion leaders may rely upon them and because they give more intensive treatment to the news, the magazines are potentially important transmitters of Supreme Court decisions. Data from Eastville and Westville supported this contention.

Viewing the presentation of the Court's action in the *Engel* and *Schempp* cases by national news magazines—*Time, Newsweek,* and *U.S. News and World Report*—we find the same general development as in the newspapers. A good deal more space was devoted to the *Engel* than to the *Schempp* decision.[41] To be sure, each of these magazines stressed the controversy which was engendered by the Court's first decision, and more space was devoted to reporting the attacks on the decision by its detractors than was given to those who supported the decision. It should be stressed once again, however, that this does not necessarily constitute bias in presentation, although that may be the impression generated. Certainly the *Engel* decision's detractors and their anguish are what made the news stories in 1962, and it is therefore reasonable that the articles should reflect this.

As pointed out, magazines present a more extensive elaboration of an issue than the newspaper or the electronics media generally. While these magazines reported the controversy, they were able to place it in perspective. The articles in all three publications carefully emphasized the limits of the *Engel* ruling; both *U.S. News* and *Time* quoted Black's footnote *in toto,* and *Time* explicitly pointed to its significance:

> Black's footnote was virtually ignored in the public reporting of the decision; it was omitted even in the text as published by the inclusive New York *Times.* Had it been given half as much attention as Douglas' sweeping dicta, much of the confusion and controversy might have been avoided.[42]

40. *Ibid.,* p. 135.

41. A comparison of space given the two cases, which includes both news articles and signed commentaries:

	Engel	*Schempp*
Newsweek	5 pages	2 pages
Time	4 pages	2 pages
U.S. News	4 pages	2 pages

42. "The Supreme Court—'To Stand as a Guarantee,'" *Time,* July 6, 1962.

The Douglas concurrence, noted in Chapter 4, tended to cast doubt on all government-financed religious exercises, no matter how tangential the financing, and the news magazines considered this to be a major factor in the ensuing controversy. David Lawrence in particular sought to allay such fears by quoting the nub of the Court's *Engel* ruling and by instructing his readers that "the foregoing quotation constitutes the ruling of the Court, and hence all other expressions of opinion are mere 'dicta.' They carry weight only as the view of individual judges." [43]

The magazines were also able to point to the source of much of the antagonism toward the Court. They noted that most of the attacks originated in the East, where school devotions were most prevalent, and among those who had previously been "losers" in cases before the Court. The prayer decision merely refueled the fires of antagonism in the coalition of Warren Court haters, as Kenneth Crawford observed in *Newsweek:*

> Part of the misunderstanding revealed by the Congressional Record had to be deliberate. Some senators and representatives from the Deep South, who are still gunning for the Court because of its school-desegregation ruling, found the school prayer decision too good an opportunity to resist. . . . Others distorted some of the Court's recent decisions to support the charge that it had defended salacious literature, drug addicts and the Communists. Several of the speakers who engaged in this distortion are lawyers who know better.[44]

The treatment given *Schempp* followed basically the same pattern as the newspaper coverage. The smaller amount of space devoted to the decision has already been noted.[45] The lack of hostile reaction was similarly noted by both *Time* and *Newsweek,* who attributed it to the fact that explicit notice was given in the majority opinion to the preferred position religion has enjoyed in American society.[46] Liberal

43. "Is Prayer in Schools Really Banned?" *U.S. News and World Report,* June 25, 1962, p. 100.

44. "The Prayer Debate," *Newsweek,* July 16, 1962, p. 28. More opposition to the Court's stand on this issue was noted in *Newsweek* than in the other news magazines. This came primarily in conservative Raymond Moley's "God, Man and Liberty," July 23, 1962, p. 76, on the *Engel* ruling; and Emmet John Hughes, "School Rooms and Prayers," July 1, 1964, p. 16, on *Schempp.*

45. See note 41, *supra.* It may be noted that magazine concern with the issue dropped generally and spectacularly from 1962 to 1963. While there were fifty article listings in the *Reader's Guide to Periodical Literature* pertaining to *Engel,* there were only nineteen for *Schempp.*

46. "Church and State," *Newsweek,* July 1, 1963, p. 48; and "The Supreme Court—A Loss to Make Up For," *Time,* June 28, 1963, p. 7.

quotations emphasizing this fact were taken from both Clark's majority opinion and Brennan's concurrence.

The only magazine to come out editorially against the Court's handling of this issue, although somewhat obliquely, was *Life*. The editors said that the *Engel* ruling collided with our spiritual heritage as a nation, a fact which they thought accounted for the popular hue and cry surrounding the decision.[47] Having predicted a "seismic" reaction if the Court followed its *Engel* precedent in the *Schempp* case,[48] *Life* acknowledged that the Court, by its explicit references in both majority and concurring opinions to the exalted position of religion in this country, took a giant stride in *Schempp* toward stifling such reaction. That *Life* still had little enthusiasm for the result was quite evident, as it noted that *Schempp,* while not weakening "our sources of moral judgment . . . certainly had not strengthened them." [49]

Little comment need be devoted to the more ideologically attuned publications with their comparatively small circulations among more or less homogeneous audiences. These magazines did not transmit the decisions in the sense that the news magazines did but rather took editorial stands on the issue consistent with their own particular frames of reference, i.e., their primary function was to reinforce their readers' commitments rather than to provide them with information. Thus the conservative and Catholic journals found themselves in opposition, while the liberal and Protestant ones generally supported the Court in both cases.[50]

• *The Specialized Publication*

Decisions and appraisals of decisions were also transmitted by publications of a more esoteric nature. Since the Supreme Court finds itself faced with problems covering the whole spectrum of social life, from legislative apportionment to contraceptives, its rulings inevitably are involved with diverse group and organizational interests. Each organization has its own channels of communication for the dissemination of

47. "A Simple Prayer Becomes a National Issue," *Life,* July 6, 1962, p. 26.

48. "The Bible—Better in School Than in Court," *Life,* March 25, 1963, p. 4.

49. "Moral Heritage and the Law," *Life,* June 28, 1963, p. 4.

50. The ideological publications represented in this analysis are the *National Review, Nation, New Republic, America, Commonweal,* and *Christian Century.* It is readily admitted that these represent a very small percentage of such materials, but they were the only ones cited in the *Reader's Guide to Periodical Literature.* A full analysis of this broad range of literature would, of course, constitute a study in itself.

information involving its central concerns. Intelligence concerning relevant Court rulings would certainly be transmitted through these same channels to those in the organization who are directly affected. Thus, important channels of transmission in the area of religious practices in schools are those that reach the participant in the field of public education. We have already treated the potential formal channel in the state educational bureaucracy, but there are others of a more general scope.

To be sure, the audience reached by specialized magazines is minute in comparison with that reached by the mass media, but Lazarsfeld and his associates found that the specialized publication was probably more important in influencing the opinion of the reader. "The specialized magazine," these writers contend,

> already has a foot in the door, so to speak, because it is accepted by the reader as a reliable spokesman for some cause or group in which he is greatly interested and with which he identifies himself. The general magazine tries to speak to everyone at once and as a result is less able to aim its shots directly at a particular target.[51]

It was suggested in interviews with school administrators in Eastville-Westville, particularly in the case of the superintendent, that specialized educational publications were important sources of information and evaluation.[52]

It is difficult to generalize about the treatment given the issue by the specialized publications studied. Some decried the lack of knowledge of what the Court actually said in the *Engel* decision. The *Educational Executives' Overview* was particularly outraged about the fact that so many "pontificated so freely" about the decision without bothering to see what the Court had said.[53] In its interpretation,

> the Court held that no government or governmental official may formulate and prescribe a prayer; hence the Regents' action was an establishment of religion in direct violation of the First Amendment. Put in these terms few would disagree. What we deplore is the kind of comment that came from our major networks and press and even from some educationists and religionists. In sweet charity let's pass over those, sworn to uphold

51. Lazarsfeld, Berelson, and Gaudet, *op. cit.*, p. 135.

52. The sources discussed in the following paragraphs were specifically noted by the superintendent or other school officials as being read by them.

53. "The Supreme Court Ruling," *Educational Executives' Overview*, August, 1962, p. 11.

the law, who rashly talked about defying it. Our outrage was at the uninformed.[54]

To counteract this knowledge gap, *Overview* printed for its readers—"responsible citizens and educational leaders"—the full majority opinion as well as "key excerpts" from the concurring and dissenting opinions.[55] In its treatment of the *Schempp* decision this magazine also was careful to emphasize the limited nature of the decision, pointing out particularly from Brennan's concurrence the indications that the decision was not antireligious. According to *Overview* the ruling merely provided "a more precise definition of what the schools can and cannot do regarding the inculcation of moral standards among young people." [56]

The *National Education Association Journal* likewise indicated that *Engel* did not bar all religious observances in public schools. It noted that the decision required further study, which it was receiving in light of a resolution passed at the 1962 N.E.A. Convention in Denver.[57] The *Journal* viewed the *Schempp* decision as more indicative of the line between permissible and impermissible religious exercises in public schools. Clark's acknowledgment of the exalted place of religion in society was noted, along with his dicta avowing the worth of an objective study of the Bible. The N.E.A. organ specifically called to the attention of "schools seeking substitutes for Bible reading and prayers" Goldberg's concurrence, which quoted Black's footnote. Such schools "may find some suggestions" for substitutions in America's historical documents, where frequent references to the Almighty are to be found.[58] Thus we see the *Journal* encouraging exercises which could be differentiated from the practices banned by the Court. It is interesting to note that it took Goldberg's concurrence a year later to bring Black's footnote to the attention of this important journal.

54. *Ibid.*
55. *Ibid.*, pp. 60, 61.
56. "High Court Strikes Down Bible and Prayer in Exercises in Public Schools," *Educational Executives' Overview*, July, 1963, p. 63. This article also noted that Finis Engelman, executive secretary of the American Association of School Administrators, sent a "lucid" memorandum to members before the decision was announced in which he correctly predicted the ultimate decision. *Overview* contended that this had a "sobering effect" on school administrators and resulted in "less morning-after confusion" than that which followed *Engel*. Hence we see other evidence of organizational channels themselves being used to transmit Court decisions.
57. "The Supreme Court Prayer Decision," *N.E.A. Journal*, October, 1962, p. 38.
58. "Supreme Court Decision on Bible Reading and Prayer Recitation," *N.E.A. Journal*, September, 1963, pp. 55–56.

The Nation's Schools viewed the *Engel* ruling as possibly the "most important court decision affecting education ever rendered." The author, who regularly covered legal questions for the publication, felt that this was just the first of a series of decisions which would surely abolish from the schools "religious practices that so many people consider a part of the spiritual heritage of this nation . . ." [59] and that it might prove to be even more significant than the school-desegregation rulings, since the latter were regional in impact while the religion-in-school issue had national scope. The author's personal dislike for the *Engel* ruling was further manifested in an article a month later in which he discussed with clear approval the manner in which the Florida Supreme Court upheld Bible-reading in that state's public schools. The Florida Court, he noted, being sensible of the extent to which agnosticism has steadily gained acceptability, was aware that religion in the schools was an effective way to offset this trend as well as to help win the struggle with Communism. The author showed obvious agreement with the Florida Court's criticism of "certain recent decisions in the field of 'religion and education,'" and with its construction of the Constitution as having a "meaning that remains constant, or static, as opposed to one that is evolving." [60] This legal writer understandably derived more satisfaction from the Court's position in the *Schempp* decision. Highlighted in his account were Clark's comments about the place of religion in society in general and the utility and desirability of an objective study of the Bible and other religious materials. Undoubtedly, the author concluded hopefully, the decision

> will provide a stimulus for including the study of religion in the public school curriculum. If the Court were not willing to support this kind of program, it's difficult to understand why it went out of its way to approve it.[61]

It is evident that the message the Court transmitted in the *Schempp* decision contained some important and reassuring elements for the writer, who in turn relayed these elements to a crucial audience.

An additional and potentially significant transmitter of Court decisions in the educational area is *School Life,* the official journal of the

59. Lee O. Garber, "Prayer Barred: What It Means," *The Nation's Schools,* August, 1962, p. 54.
60. Garber, "Florida Bible Case Asks: Do Majorities Have Rights, Too?" *The Nation's Schools,* September, 1962, pp. 110–11.
61. Garber, "Bible Reading Out, But Religion May Be In for Public Schools," *The Nation's Schools,* August, 1963, p. 51.

U.S. Office of Education. This was not seen by any administrator in Eastville-Westville, although the superintendent did volunteer that he attended a school administrators' conference at which a representative of the Office of Education explained and interpreted the earlier ruling. The articles included in *School Life* may be classified as neutral transmitters of what the Court has said, since most of them consist of quotations, with little independent interpretation.[62] The Office perceives itself as a collector and disseminator of information about education, including its legal aspects. It does not, however, give legal advice to school administrators, although it answers inquiries. Such answers often include reprints of articles which have appeared in *School Life*.[63]

• *Summary*

Considerable space has been devoted to a discussion of the multiple channels through which Court decisions are transmitted to the locale of implementation. Formal legal-political channels are of crucial importance to the Supreme Court decisional structure as a whole, but these channels are primarily limited to those relatively few instances where formal litigation is involved. Broad-scale compliance, as we have seen, necessitates implementing activities well beyond the normal confines of the legal process with its court orders, law reports, and formal opinions.[64]

Compliance with Supreme Court decisions may occur as individuals who occupy a variety of positions throughout society learn about the decisions and feel "pressured" to ensure that their behavior as well as that of others is congruent with Court policy. This may result, as we have contended in Chapter 2, when mere knowledge of Court decisions is brought into proximity with knowledge of related ongoing social processes.

It is important, therefore, to reflect upon the many ways in which

62. See, for example, August W. Steinhilber, "Supreme Court Decision on Government-Sponsored Prayer," *School Life*, July, 1962, pp. 8–9; and "Bible Reading in the Public Schools," *School Life*, October, 1963, pp. 13–16.

63. Letter to the author from Francis Keppel, U.S. Commissioner of Education, June 5, 1964.

64. Another possible channel of a formal nature is the law review. This was not relevant as far as Eastville-Westville was concerned and thus was not investigated. Needless to say, the treatment given the Court's rulings in the religion-in-public-schools area by the reviews is extensive, and a systematic evaluation would be a separate study.

knowledge of Court policy gets to the level of implementation and to investigate the adequacy of this transmission. As far as Eastville-Westville is concerned, there is not a shred of evidence suggesting that the formal legal channels were of significance in the transmission of information about the Court's policies. Yet the policy was implemented. The newspapers, radio and TV, and magazines were the principal means by which the word filtered down to this community. Focusing upon the coverage given the Court's action by these channels, we have seen that the conscientious observer had ample opportunity to be apprised of the Court's policies and the reasoning behind them. But the more casual observer might have received a partial and somewhat distorted view of what the Court had said, particularly with respect to the *Engel* decision. By the same token, ample opportunity was presented to the observer who had a commitment on the issue, as he could selectively expose himself to materials which would tend to reinforce his commitment.

Even though one might acknowledge the limitations of the mass media as transmitters of Supreme Court messages, the Court is not powerless in coping with the situation. As the treatment given by the various media to the *Schempp* ruling demonstrates, a concern with message *clarity* by the Court improves the chances for adequate transmission. It appears that, by going to great lengths to express the limitations of the ruling, the Court was able to get much more positive treatment by the media. It might again be suggested that it is helpful for the Court to take special pains to grant symbolic rewards to widely respected interests, especially in instances where substantive rewards are being withheld.[65] In *Schempp* the Court took care of both these aspects. As Chapter 4 demonstrated, the opinion for the majority explicitly noted which religious activities were prohibited and which were not touched by the decision. Additionally, the esteemed place of religion in American society was specifically acknowledged. These points were not lost on the nation's reporters, editors, and commentators.

65. On this point see Murray Edelman, *The Symbolic Uses of Politics* (Urbana: University of Illinois Press, 1964), Chapter 2, "Symbols and Political Quiescence."

CHAPTER 7

Eastville–Westville: Setting and Reaction

THE SETTING within which a message is received is another crucial variable in a communication situation.[1] Two aspects of the relevant setting will be considered in this chapter, first, the characteristics of the Eastville-Westville district—the milieu penetrated by the Court's messages—and second, the institutional setting of relevance to the Court's rulings—the public school apparatus.

• Eastville-Westville

The Eastville-Westville Community Unit school district is situated in the midst of the fertile farm lands of central Illinois. The district consists of the two small villages, of nearly equal population (450 each), and the surrounding countryside; there are less than 2,000 residents in the district as a whole. The two villages are some five miles apart and are linked by a second-class state highway.

The towns, with their limited commercial facilities, only partially service the environs. Each town has its bank, grain elevators, food markets, and other small retail and service facilities, but certain larger cities in the area, such as Decatur and Champaign, perform the principal service functions. The villages, however, exist as the focal points for the social life of the locale. This activity centers about the church.

The Methodist Church, because of the size and importance of its congregation, is the principal church in both villages. There is a

1. Carl I. Hovland, Irving L. Janis, and Harold H. Kelley, *Communication and Persuasion* (New Haven: Yale University Press, 1953).

relatively large Christian Church in Eastville, and it is the only church—other than Methodist—in either community that has a resident pastor. Each town has a small Baptist Church which serves individuals who are not closely identified with the community.

The religious facet is highly visible in the life of the community. One becomes quite aware of this as he walks down the business street in Westville and observes the posters in the shop windows which proclaim the evils of alcohol and nicotine and suggest that they represent the antithesis of Jesus Christ. The posters are the product of an annual contest sponsored by the locally powerful Woman's Christian Temperance Union. Questionnaire responses further substantiate the impression that religion is considered important for a great many in this locality. Part of these data are summarized in Table 6. One sees that substantial percentages of the respondents are members of churches, attend services, and participate to a considerable extent. Many indicate that religion is of very great importance in their lives. This impression was reinforced numerous times in interviews with school officials and community leaders, who were not reticent about their religious convictions.

TABLE 6

Religious Profile of Eastville-Westville Respondents

Church membership:		*Denomination:*	
Member	85%	Methodist	55%
Nonmember	15	Disciples of Christ	19
Extent of church participation: [b]		Baptist	10
Very much	24%	Other [a]	14
Average	40	None	2
Not much	18	*Church attendance:* [b]	
None	17	Once a week or more	56%
Importance of religion compared with other activities:		2 or 3 times per month	14
More important	52%	Once a month or less	24
Same	30	None	5
Less important	18		

[a] "Other" denominations include Evangelical United Brethren, Catholic, and Lutheran.

[b] Percentages do not total to 100 because of rounding.

The Methodist Church not only has the greatest number of members in each town, but it also includes those individuals who reputedly "count." Those who make up both the visible and invisible government of the two towns are, by and large, Methodists. At the time of this study such an affiliation was nearly a prerequisite for a position on the school board, where all but one member was a Methodist. The deviant was a Lutheran, but he had attended the local Methodist church for some years and was married to one of its members. The former president of the school board was the long-time superintendent of the Eastville Methodist Church's Sunday school, while another member of the school board was the chairman of the board of this church. The former school superintendent taught the adult Sunday-school class in the Westville church. The present superintendent, while not a member, attended the Methodist Church in Westville. A number of the schoolteachers in the district doubled as teachers in the Sunday schools.

Both of the Methodist ministers were reported to be in rather precarious positions vis-à-vis their congregations. The ministers, who were assigned to the churches by the denominational hierarchy, were accused by some of introducing alien ideas into the religious life of the community. The present school-board president, a man of Fundamentalist religious preferences, volunteered that the ministers had been trained in "liberal" seminaries, where they were allegedly taught that parts of the Bible are mere legend and not the literal truth. The church hierarchy was further accused of "compelling" the ministers to repeat a certain "line" from the pulpit. This line was characterized as feebly representative of the theology which is meaningful to many in the community. The commitment was to a local church, expressive of a rather traditional and Fundamentalist brand of religion which fortifies one against the forces of secularism in the outside world.[2]

The Westville Women's Christian Temperance Union was a powerful force in the community. This group, composed primarily of Methodist women, traditionally had a considerable degree of access to the schools of the community. Not only did the W.C.T.U. conduct the poster contest we have mentioned, but they sponsored essay contests as well, the themes of which emphasized the merits of temperance. The

2. The state university was the target of some gibes in the interviews as respondents related some of the evil things "taught" their children in college, which were certainly a far cry from the teachings of their community and its church!

W.C.T.U. also conducted lectures and showed movies during school hours, along with supplying the schools with abundant temperance literature.

It is important to note the convergence of religious life and education in the community. There was the interlocking of directorates in the community religious and educational establishments as board members and teachers occupied official roles in the religious organizations of the community. Beyond this, the informal, interpersonal communications network in the community closely tied the two establishments together, as we shall see later. The highly visible activity of the W.C.T.U. in injecting moral values into the school curriculum was still another manifestation of this interweaving of religion and education in Eastville-Westville.

The educational structure is the sole linkage between Eastville and Westville. On the surface the two localities seem to have much in common. They are of comparable size, have similar economic interests centering around agriculture, and their social life revolves around the Methodist Church. Nevertheless, there is little communication between the two villages. In fact, the residents apparently perceive that a sizable social gulf exists between the two places. The author was frequently asked rhetorically, in the course of interviews, whether he had sensed the vast differences between the two towns. The Westvillians, in particular, see the differences in class terms. Westville, they say, is primarily a homogeneous, middle-class community in which the people find it easy to "get along" with one another. Eastville, on the other hand, is viewed as containing a sharp cleavage between the upper class and the lower class that permeates the society and reaches even into the church. Some Eastvillians, on the other hand, expressed antagonism toward the activities of the Westville W.C.T.U. No qualitative difference between residents of the two towns was observed in the questionnaire responses, however.

The public education system officially draws the two localities together, but the gap noted above has not been successfully bridged and was reported to be one factor lying behind the dismissal of the former superintendent, who was predominantly identified with the Westville community. His successor, who comes from outside the system, has made a concerted effort to close the gap. For instance, the superintendent placed much emphasis on getting the new high-school principal a residence in Eastville to help offset the fact that the other principals and the superintendent himself all resided in Westville. A rebirth of the defunct Parent-Teacher Association was also viewed as a way of more tightly integrating the principal elements of the school district.

• *The School System*

The second relevant aspect of the setting is the local public educational system, the institutional arrangement most directly affected by the Court's prayer decisions. Since 1948 the Eastville and Westville school systems have been merged into a single community unit system. At the time of our study, a total of 34 teachers and administrators served a clientele of approximately 260 families and 600 students in the Eastville-Westville district. Each village has its own grade school (kindergarten through sixth grade), while the junior high school (grades seven through nine) is located in Westville. In the country, nearly equidistant from the two villages, is the unit high school. This school, of very recent construction, is modern and well equipped and is viewed with uniform pride by the residents of the district.

The local school system consists of four primary interrelated positions—the school-board member, the superintendent, the principal, and the teacher. The school board—or the board of education, as it is officially labeled—is the governing body of the system. Its members are chosen in staggered annual elections for three-year terms. The district board, at the time of this study, consisted of six farmers and the proprietor of the Westville grain elevator. The latter member had been selected by his colleagues as chairman of the board for a one-year period.

Officially, policy is made for the local school system by this board; its responsibilities and obligations are fairly well spelled out in the Illinois School Code.[3] Its most important responsibilities include raising sufficient funds to run the schools, budgeting, reviewing curricula, overseeing the repair and maintenance of the physical facilities, and obtaining personnel. In actuality, its most important function is to hire the district superintendent, who provides day-to-day leadership in the system.

Technically, the superintendent acts under the direction of the board; in fact, the policy-making function is shared by the board and its superintendent. This has a statutory basis in the School Code,

3. *Illinois Revised Statutes,* 1961, Chap. 122, sec. 10-10, p. 1929.

which provides that "the Superintendent shall make recommendations to the board concerning the budget, building plans, the location of sites, the selection of teachers, instructional materials and courses of study." [4] This is a necessary arrangement. The superintendent is brought into the system as *the* educational expert, qualified by both training and experience. He has a background superior to most on the board for dealing with the array of quite technical problems which arise. Consequently, a major share of policy-making devolves on the superintendent, while the board retains the reins of policy-making by ratifying the policies generated by the superintendent. This was obviously the case in Eastville-Westville; some members openly acknowledged that their prior experience had ill-prepared them for the range of problems arising in the operation of an educational system. The efforts of the superintendent in providing over-all leadership was both appreciated and expected by the board.

The superintendent is the formal link between the board and those entrusted with the immediate responsibility of educating the district's youth—the school principals and teachers. He presides over unit teachers meetings, has frequent meetings with his principals, and interacts frequently on a more informal day-to-day basis with the personnel of the system. Thus there is a multiplicity of arrangements through which he conveys policy to occupants of important positions in the school system. But while the superintendent is the formal link between the board and the educational staff, in Eastville-Westville the process can easily be short-circuited. The superintendent and the formal systemic channels are frequently bypassed as school-board members and teachers interact socially, allowing for the exchange of expectations, whether or not such exchange is intentional. The church in particular provides an opportunity for such contacts.

It is the superintendent, of course, who provides the chief link between the local school system and the larger educational world. He relates the local system to the state educational hierarchy, as most directives from above come to him for action, and he originates most communications from the local system to higher authority. He has major responsibility for ensuring that the district schools conform to the expectations of the state educational establishment. In addition, he relates the system to a variety of groups and organizations of a professional nature. Multiple specialized publications convey a set of

4. *Ibid.*, sec. 10-21.4, p. 1932.

professional expectations to the superintendent which may in turn be introduced into the system by him. Others in the system, such as the teachers and principals, have external professional connections, but the superintendent is in the best position to bring these views to bear in the formulation of over-all policy.

Others in the community, although not occupying formal systemic roles, are directly relevant to the operation of the school system. There is, for instance, the clientele group which entrusts the education of its youth to the school officials and teachers—the school-district parents. Parents may communicate expectations concerning the operation of the schools through multiple channels. Parent-Teacher associations and similar organizations traditionally provide formal means of doing so, and frequent less formal interaction between parents and teachers and administrators is often encouraged. In Eastville-Westville the P.T.A. had passed out of existence because of lack of interest on the part of the parents. Perhaps the frequency of informal social interaction between board members, teachers, and parents made such formal activity seem unnecessary. The superintendent reported that the parents of Eastville-Westville were quite reluctant to deal directly with his office. Thus he was interested in re-establishing the P.T.A. as a channel of communication between himself and the parents, since he had not as yet become "plugged into" the informal social network.

Influential citizens in the district, whether or not they are the parents of schoolchildren, often take an active interest in certain facets of school policy and are viewed as quite important by school administrators. The importance of the "influential" has been pressed upon the administrator through his specialized publications. An article in *Educational Executives' Overview,* for instance, discussed this notion and suggested that no school administrator

> can discharge his leadership responsibility adequately until he is able to relate himself effectively to the community decision-making process, and a decisive element in the process is the informal power structure within the community.[5]

As will be discussed more fully in the next chapter, this stratum is important for the general transmission of information and evaluation

5. Archie Dykes, "Face to Face with the Power Elite," *Educational Executives' Overview* (May 1963), p. 34. Arthur J. Vidich and Joseph Bensman (*Small Town in Mass Society* [Garden City: Doubleday & Co., Inc., 1958]) do a creditable job of demonstrating the relationship between the educational apparatus and "significant others" in the community of "Springdale."

to those in the community who are relatively less exposed. Matters relating to education are no exceptions in this regard. Consequently, knowing the thoughts and expectations of these individuals is of crucial concern to the school administrator. The superintendent of the Eastville-Westville district was not unmindful of this. Being relatively new on the scene, he was actively engaged in ascertaining the "power structure" of the district and viewed our study as a possible aid in this regard. As we shall see in the next chapter, community influentials did indeed play a significant role in support of the superintendent's action with respect to the implementation of Supreme Court policy.

Since we have specified the positions included in or relevant to the local educational system principally in terms of their relationships with the superintendent, we should concentrate, at this point, on the incumbent of this focal position. At the time of this study, the superintendent was in his first year in Eastville-Westville. A man in his mid-thirties, the superintendent had moved to the central Illinois community from Ohio, where he had taught and had been a school administrator in three different rural school districts. He had a master's degree and aspired to the doctorate. Hence he decided to seek a superintendency near a major graduate school where he could eventually pursue course work in addition to his administrative duties. He would have preferred to obtain a Ph.D. in the field of economics and ultimately to teach at the college level; however, his previous graduate work in education, his responsibilities as the head of a family, and a perceived adverse age factor all seemed to indicate that further academic work should be in the field of education.

In many respects the superintendent was set apart from others in the community. At least in his first year, his contacts in the community were primarily associated with his role. He spoke on occasion of this isolation—of having "nobody to talk to"—and enjoyed the informal contacts with the author while the field work for this study was being conducted. It was a difficult first year for the new administrator, for he had not only to handle the administrative chores but also to come to grips with the workings of the school system; he could turn to no one directly for information and advice concerning many dimensions of life in Eastville-Westville.

The superintendent was further set apart from the community in terms of his personal interests. He was not a member of the local Methodist Church, although he did attend. In this sense he differed from his predecessor, who taught the adult Sunday-school class in the

Westville Methodist Church, a crucial point in the web of social interactions in the community. In addition, the superintendent was quite cosmopolitan in his orientations. He classified himself as a "reader" and found few in the community who shared this avocation. The superintendent and his wife frequently journeyed to Champaign to partake of the cultural life associated with the University of Illinois. This activity was alien to most in the community; such behavior was considered a bit "strange." These cosmopolitan orientations of the superintendent take on added significance as we study the impingement of the Court's prayer rulings on Eastville-Westville.

• *The Supreme Court and Eastville-Westville*

Recent Court rulings involving religious practices in public schools present a potential disturbance to ongoing processes in educational systems throughout the land. There are two necessary conditions which determine whether or not such policies do in fact constitute a disturbance to a system. The first has to do with the relevance of the Court's rulings to practices in the system. Certainly, the Court's holdings proscribing prayers and Bible reading in public schools have no relevance for those systems in which such practices do not take place. As far as the system as a whole is concerned, there is no disturbance.

Second, there must be an awareness of the rulings on the part of those in relevant positions in the system. Practices identical to those determined to be unconstitutional in the *Schempp* ruling may take place in a local educational system, yet, if there is a lack of awareness, particularly on the part of role-players directly involved with them, it is unlikely that the system will be disturbed.

Once these two conditions—relevance and awareness by crucial role-players—have been met, Supreme Court interpretation may have a very direct impact on a local system even where linkages between the Court and the community via formal legal channels are entirely lacking.

Who these "crucial role-players" are may vary from system to system, although any of the roles of the system may be involved. The superintendent and the school board as the primary policy-making core of the local educational system, the principals as less important policy-makers, or the teacher who actually leads the class in the proscribed exercise are all in a position to implement the Court's policy. If awareness of the ruling on the part of these actors causes an imbalance when considered in connection with current practices, the balance may be restored in a number of ways: the practices may be brought into conformity with the Court's determination; the superintendent or the board may issue a general stop order; the principal may order his teachers to desist; or the individual teacher may on his own discontinue the banned practices in his classroom.

We suggested in Chapter 2 that behavioral change is not the only mode of resolution for imbalance. Problems of imbalance may be met on the cognitive level as well. The classroom teacher or the principal may consider that any behavioral change must come from directives by those higher up in the system, while the board and its superintendent may in turn "await" specific directives from the state office. Similarly, any of these role-players may absolve themselves of personal responsibility by differentiating what they do in their schools from the practices—conducted elsewhere—which were declared unconstitutional. The modes of *denial* and *transcendence,* both discussed in Chapter 2, may also be used to attack the Court and/or its ruling as a justification for perpetuating the status quo. The point is that, even in a small and inclusive social system such as a local educational establishment, there are a number of roles which are components in a system of Supreme Court decision-making, and whether or not a ruling by the Court is an *effective* policy depends to a large extent upon how these actors resolve their role-associated dilemmas.

Both school-prayer rulings impinged upon the Eastville-Westville school district, at least in the minds of certain of the actors. The practices which some considered to be departures from those constitutionally acceptable were formal prayers said in the elementary schools' cafeterias prior to lunch. It was common for a student selected by the teacher to lead the class in a prayer which, on occasion, was composed by the teacher. Some teachers in the lower grades, it was reported, also had prayers in the classroom as part of a morning devotional exercise. Other religious practices held in the district schools, but not generally perceived as coming under the Court's ban, were annual baccalaureate services held in the high school, traditional Christmas and Easter programs, distribution of Gideon Bibles, and certain of the activities sponsored by the W.C.T.U.

After the *Engel* ruling the principal of the Eastville grade school went to the superintendent, the incumbent's predecessor, and contended that certain of these practices should be stopped. The superintendent, an active participant in the Westville church, advised the principal that in a Methodist community such as this it was best to turn one's head away from certain things. "Don't jeopardize your job," he was told. Others had asked the superintendent whether the *Engel* ruling would apply to the lunch-time prayers, and he responded in the negative, differentiating the local practices from those held unconstitutional. The school officials would never do away with the prayers before lunch, this superintendent reported telling people, "unless a policeman was put at the door." Reportedly, church and civic organizations in the community agreed with the stand taken by the superintendent. In this instance dominant values in the community, as perceived by and congruent with those of a central decision-maker, were sufficient to offset any knowledge of relevant Supreme Court policy. In actuality, *Engel v. Vitale* brought little disturbance to the system.

The summer following the *Schempp* ruling saw an important personnel change in the Eastville-Westville school system, as the superintendent was replaced. The new superintendent brought with him some experience concerning religious practices in the public schools. In previous positions in Ohio he served in one small community which was dominated by Methodists, while, in another, 70 per cent of the population was Catholic, nuns taught in the public schools, and students were regularly released from school for religious instruction. This background was an important element in shaping his response to the set of circumstances he found in his new position.

To the new superintendent, the Court's rulings on religious practices in public schools were "right," expressive of his own values. Youngsters in the elementary grades are very pliable, he explained, and it was not the function of the public schools to "indoctrinate" them in terms of religion. This, he felt, was the function of the church. He applied a rather rigid standard of constitutionality. His understanding of the Court's policy—gained primarily from attending a conference at which a representative of the U.S. Office of Education spoke—was that *neutrality* between religious denominations was not enough. Rather, there should be *no establishment* of religion in the public schools. The prayer before lunch in the school cafeterias was interpreted by him to be an "establishment of religion."

Coming into the system with this awareness of the Court's treatment of the issue and with this set of personal views, the superintendent soon became aware of the religious practices in the schools. His response to the imbalance was to change the ongoing behavior. On three occasions he informally mentioned to the principals of the elementary schools that the practice of formal prayer before lunch should be stopped. According to the superintendent, the first suggestion was embodied, somewhat obliquely, in a hint. The next two references were framed in more direct and stronger language. Finally, in a unit teachers' meeting his position was stated to the principals and teachers alike. Here the superintendent referred to the Court's policy on religious practices in schools and asserted that the practice of lunch-time prayers in the school cafeterias ran counter to this policy. It was reported that in his admonition the superintendent stated that he could not support teachers involved if trouble arose over the continuation of such practices.

This more formal articulation of the superintendent's expectations brought the desired compliance. The Eastville principal on the next day circulated the following memorandum to his teachers:

> Starting today there will be no more organized forms of prayer in the lunch room or on school premises.
>
> If, however, individuals in your room would care to say a silent prayer at lunch the other people at the table should show courtesy in this matter and remain silent. That is all that is required of them.[6]

The behavior of the Eastville principal is most interesting. Recall that he had urged the former superintendent to take action in light of the *Engel* ruling. In the present instance, however, he did not act at the superintendent's initial behest but waited until the superintendent had publicly stated his position in the unit teachers' meeting. In this way he was able to promulgate the order to his teachers while the superintendent was placed in a position of assuming responsibility for such action. The Eastville principal explained that he had to live and work with his teachers—who were highly committed to the religious practices—and thus needed to establish the superintendent as a scapegoat.

Even in this system we see operative the notion of a "hierarchy of scapegoats," discussed earlier. The superintendent was here perceived to be in a better position than the principal for implementing the ruling of the Court. The principal's contact with the teachers and the parents of Eastville was more intimate, while the superintendent enjoyed a measure of "social distance" with respect to both teachers and parents. The superintendent also acknowledged that, had trouble been encountered in this community as a result of his ruling, he would have

6. Memorandum of October 21, 1963.

consulted the state office for an interpretation. Appeal to the top educational officer in the state existed as another potential stage in this hierarchy of scapegoats.

The Court, standing at the apex of this hierarchy, performed the crucial function of legitimizing the superintendent's action. With no Court policy on the subject, the superintendent admitted, he would not have taken the action, even though he was opposed to the ongoing practices. Because of the Court's *Engel* and *Schempp* rulings, the superintendent was able to carry out a policy which flew in the face of the dominant values of the community as well as those held by many in the educational system itself, without a word of criticism reaching his ears.[7]

This is not to say that some accommodations were not made. As the directive promulgated by the Eastville principal indicates, the verbal prayers in the cafeterias were replaced by silent ones, while other practices, such as baccalaureate services and W.C.T.U. activities, continued. Perhaps these accommodations were sufficient to prevent the issue from assuming huge proportions in the community. Other explanations will be presented below. Nevertheless, the action was sufficient to bring existing programs into perceived compliance with the Court's rulings as far as the central decision-maker for the system was concerned. To him, the impressionable school child was not forcibly exposed to the religious preferences of others in the schools of the community, which, to him, was the gist of the Court's position.

7. The board of education was not apprised of the superintendent's action of some five months before until the superintendent informed the members in conjunction with an announcement that the author had interviewed him and would be seeking interviews with them.

CHAPTER 8

The Structure of Response

THE ENUNCIATION of Supreme Court policy in the *Engel* and *Schempp* cases creates a new set of role obligations for actors in educational systems, although such obligations are not always recognized or acknowledged. In the Eastville-Westville school district the superintendent did recognize some degree of obligation; he acted and thereby became a component in a rather loosely coordinated system of Supreme Court decision-making.

Role analysis suggests that actors behave with reference to the expectations of others.[1] The crucial role-definers or "role others" in this particular instance were not found within the system. Rather, the superintendent looked beyond the boundaries of the system for reference. He drew upon his past experience concerning religious influences in the public schools and viewed the Court's policy as one which stated the best possible arrangement between religion and education. As opposed to this, the former superintendent admittedly looked within the system for definition of his role in shaping the district's response, or perhaps nonresponse, to the Court's ruling in the *Engel* case. In both instances, however, "role others" at the local level had a part to play. It was more direct in the case of the former superintendent's handling of the issue. In the more recent instance, "role others" greeted the new superintendent's directive with at least acquiescence; there was no public indication that the superintendent had performed his role incorrectly.

1. See, for example, Neal Gross, Ward S. Mason, and Alexander W. McEachern, *Explorations in Role Analysis: Studies of the School Superintendency Role* (New York: John Wiley & Sons, Inc., 1958), and Erving Goffman, "Role Distance," in *Encounters: Two Studies in the Sociology of Interaction* (Indianapolis: Bobbs-Merrill Co., Inc., 1961).

From what has been stated previously, this acquiescence on the part of members in the community might appear surprising. The community is very patently a religious one, and the public school system was not unaffected by this religiosity. The lunch-time prayer was just one of its manifestations. In interviews, respondent after respondent indicated that the prayers were held because they were expressive of the desires of the community. The superintendent, who was immediately responsible for the discontinuance of the lunch-time prayers, expressed surprise that his action had not stirred a community controversy. In fact, he had received no protest to his action from either teacher or parent. Similarly, the Eastville grade-school principal had expected repercussions. Though these had not yet been forthcoming, he confidently predicted that the study being conducted by the author would ignite the fuse of popular protest. The issue was lying dormant, he said, but the questionnaire would start people thinking about what had happened to a desirable, even imperative, exercise in their schools. This study did not activate latent hostility, however, as the community continued peacefully to accept the superintendent's policy.

It might be argued that their acquiescence perhaps stemmed from the fact that most of the people in this community personally accepted and agreed with what the Supreme Court had said about prayers in the public school. According to questionnaire responses, however, this was not the case. Only a quarter of the Eastville-Westville respondents reported that they personally agreed with the Court's handling of the relevant cases.[2] Indeed, over 70 per cent of the respondents felt that the Court had exceeded its range of power in this matter; fewer than 20 per cent acknowledged that the issue was one properly to be handled by the Court.[3] For a majority, the Court's *Engel* and *Schempp* rulings were viewed as assisting feared "Godless groups" [4] and fitted a "general trend in this country toward Godlessness, corruption, crime, divorce, and delinquency." [5]

2. Questionnaire item 27: "Do you agree or disagree with what the Court has said about religious practices in public schools?" Agree: 25.6%; Disagree: 52.3%; No opinion: 22.2%. For the full interview schedule see Appendix B.

3. Item 35: "Although the Court should interpret the Constitution, it has gone too far when it starts telling us that we can't pray in our schools." Agree: 71.0%; Disagree: 19.3%; No opinion: 9.7%.

4. Item 40: "The problem with these decisions is that they aid undesirable Godless groups." Agree: 58.5%; Disagree: 19.3%; No opinion: 22.2%.

5. Item 48: "These decisions may seem harmless, but they fit into the general trend in this country toward Godlessness, corruption, crime, divorce, and delinquency." Agree: 53.4%; Disagree: 31.8%; No opinion: 14.8%.

Despite this lack of personal acceptance of the rulings and their negative implications, half of the respondents acknowledged the necessity for public compliance with them.[6] It is obvious, then, that private acceptance and public compliance are, for many persons, distinct factors. If we consider the community response from the perspective of the public-compliance dimension, the lack of controversy following the superintendent's announced policy is more comprehensible.

Of more importance, however, is the *distribution* of attitudes supportive of public compliance. A sizable majority of those actors who are

TABLE 7

Roles Compared as to Whether or Not a Duty of Public Compliance Is Recognized

System Roles	Public Compliers	Non-compliers	Totals
Teachers [a]	17	7	24
School board	5	2	7
Influentials [b]	21	13	34

[a] Includes the superintendent and principals.
[b] This category includes some teachers and board members as well as others.

most actively involved in the school system and in community affairs in general acknowledged the duty of public compliance. The principal roles of the system are compared in Table 7 as to their recognition of a public duty to comply. It is clear from this table that there was a sound foundation of support for the superintendent's action among people who "count."

What this community expects of the school official in his role as a component of the compliance process has heretofore been discussed in very general terms. The preceding paragraphs have indicated that in the final analysis the majority of those most directly involved in Eastville-Westville expected compliance with the Court rulings. Precisely what does compliance entail, however? Does compliance with the

6. Item 34: "No matter what one may think about religious practices, if the Supreme Court says they are unconstitutional, one has the duty to accept the decision and act accordingly." Agree: 50.0%; Disagree: 40.9%; No opinion: 9.1%. This question is used throughout as the index of public compliance, that is, the recognition of a duty to ensure that public activity is in compliance with Supreme Court policy. Those who recognize the duty of public compliance are variously referred to as "public compliers."

Schempp ruling mean the abandonment of all religious activity in the schools? Because our research was conducted so many months after the issue had arisen, this question could not be studied directly, and it was decided to pose an extreme hypothetical case and ask the respondents to indicate what specific action they would expect from their school officials in light of a relevant Court ruling. The question (Number 26 in the questionnaire) was: "If the Supreme Court would declare unconstitutional Christmas programs in public schools, what do you feel your local school officials should do about such programs in your

TABLE 8

Role Expectations of Public Compliers and Noncompliers

Item 26: "If the Supreme Court would declare unconstitutional Christmas programs in public schools, what do you feel your local school officials should do about such programs in your schools?"

	Action Expectations				
Public Compliance	Stop Programs	No Action	Order to Continue	Substitute Arrangement	Totals
Agree	17	14	12	33	76
Disagree	3	23	16	22	64
Totals	20	37	28	55	140

schools?" Four action alternatives were presented for the respondent's choice: (1) Order a stop. (2) Take no action. (3) Order programs to continue. (4) Draw up a substitute arrangement to satisfy both religious as well as legal needs. An open-ended "other action" category was also offered, but it produced no insightful alternative. The results of this probe, cross-tabulated with the public-compliance dimension, are presented in Table 8. A qualitative difference in responses can be observed between those who do and those who do not recognize a general obligation to comply. The noncompliers disproportionately preferred the expectations which in fact would constitute noncompliant behavior, i.e., taking no action at all or even ordering programs to continue despite the ruling. Similarly, the public compliers disproportionately preferred specific actions which can be construed as compliant, i.e., to stop the programs or to devise suitable and "legal" alternatives.[7] The differences between the groups on these action categories is statistically

7. Of the twenty respondents expecting officials to stop such programs, thirteen are individuals who also agree privately with the rulings as well as expect public compliance.

significant at the .01 level, according to the Chi-square test. While there is an element of redundancy here—compliers expect compliant action and vice versa—this is useful for pointing out the precise kinds of action these categories of respondents expected from their school officials.[8] It is to be noted that a sizable proportion of both the compliers and noncompliers preferred the fourth alternative, which was to devise a suitable substitute arrangement which conceivably could be defended both legally and religiously and which could be "differentiated" from the practices declared unconstitutional. Herein lies another possible source of support for the action taken by the superintendent in the wake of the *Schempp* ruling. While the verbal prayer before lunch was discontinued, the pause for a silent prayer was recognized. A complete indifference to the religious character of the community was thus avoided. Beyond this, other religious activities have been allowed to continue in the school's baccalaureate services, Christmas programs, and W.C.T.U.–sponsored exercises. The community seemed to be satisfied, since nearly 49 per cent of the respondents indicated approval of action taken by their officials, while only 16 per cent disapproved, the remaining respondents having no opinion either way.[9] In light of these factors, community acceptance of the superintendent's action becomes more comprehensible.

• The Influentials

The concept of the "influentials" was introduced in the previous chapter as an important concern of the superintendent. In this chapter we have noted that the influentials seemed to provide an important support for the superintendent's action, since a sizable majority of them were found in the public-compliance category. It is much to the point, then, to take a careful look at these influentials, for they appear to be a crucial element in the structure of response.

Studies in recent years have indicated the importance and efficacy of the informal, impersonal types of communication. It was demonstrated

8. It may be considered inconsistent that some "public compliers" would expect "no action" or "order action to continue" in this instance, neither of which would constitute compliance. Conceivably this discrepancy could be attributed to the extreme nature of the hypothetical case. There are obviously limits to the range of Supreme Court power, and possibly for some these limits were exceeded in this instance.

9. Item 24: "How would you describe your feelings about the way your school officials have handled the question of religion in school?"

in *The People's Choice* that personal contact was more effective than exposure to the mass media for opinion change.[10] Certain individuals—variously referred to as "opinion leaders" or "influentials"—tend to expose themselves to the formal media to a greater extent than others, and ideas tend to flow from print or from the electronics media to them and thence to less active segments of the population. This has been referred to as the "two-step flow of communication." [11]

The concept of the influentials is significant from two points of view. One, as just noted, involves the flow of information wherein the influentials perform a "relay" function. Second, the influentials *evaluate* information received from multiple sources and relay their evaluations to the less well informed. Consequently, the influentials are conveyors of values as well. They provide frames of reference through which others may formulate attitudes toward aspects of their environment and standards by which individuals may evaluate themselves.[12]

There are certain essential characteristics which allow the influentials to perform both a communicative and reference role. First, influence seems to be related to the personification of certain values. That is to say, individuals are accorded influential status because they exemplify and/or articulate acceptable values. Second, influentials are viewed as competent; they are perceived as knowing what they are talking about. Third, they are perceived to occupy what may be called "strategic social location." That is, they have access to a wide range of media relevant to their domain of influence, as well as relevant personal contacts with the outside world.[13]

We would be remiss, therefore, to neglect this factor in the present context. As has been stressed, compliance with a Supreme Court decision is unattainable unless the order is transmitted to those who are under obligation to act. The influentials, as many studies have indi-

10. Paul Lazarsfeld, Bernard Berelson, and Hazel Gaudet, *The People's Choice* (New York: Duell, Sloan & Pearce, 1945).

11. Elihu Katz and Paul F. Lazarsfeld, *Personal Influence* (Glencoe: The Free Press, 1955).

12. See, for example, Herbert Hyman, "The Psychology of Status," *Archives of Psychology,* No. 269 (1942), Chap. IV, and Hyman, "Reflections on Reference Groups," 24 *Public Opinion Quarterly* 383 (1960). See also Robert K. Merton, "Continuities in the Theory of Reference Groups and Social Structure," and Robert K. Merton and Alice S. Rossi, "Contributions to the Theory of Reference Group Behavior," in Merton (ed.), *Social Theory and Social Structure* (Glencoe: The Free Press, 1957), pp. 281–386 and 225–80, respectively.

13. Arthur J. Vidich and Joseph Bensman, *Small Town in Mass Society* (Garden City: Doubleday & Co., Inc., 1958), pp. 88 ff.

cated, are an important component in any communication system, and here one would expect no exception. One would expect the influentials to play a significant role in the transmission of Supreme Court decisions as well as in establishing a normative standard by which the rulings of the Court are evaluated. Thus, broad-range acceptance of Supreme Court decisions is in large part dependent upon acceptance by these individuals.

The indicator of personal influence employed in this study is a questionnaire item which involved the "self-designation of opinion leadership."[14] Here respondents were asked: "Compared with other

TABLE 9

Occupations of Self-designated Influentials

	Influential	Noninfluential	*N*
Farmers	6 (9.5%)	57 (90.5%)	63
Business, clerical, and sales	5 (27.8)	13 (72.2)	18
Teachers	17 (65.3)	9 (34.7)	26
Professionals and civil servants	2 (28.6)	5 (71.4)	7
Housewives	5 (15.2)	28 (84.8)	33
Workmen	1 (4.1%)	23 (95.9%)	24
Totals	36 (21%)	135 (79%)	171 (100%)

people you know, are you more or less likely to be asked for information or advice about these matters (Court decisions involving religious practices in the schools)?" Slightly over 20 per cent of the respondents designated themselves as being more likely to be asked in this regard. Our analysis will concentrate upon these self-designated influentials as we seek to define their characteristics and to compare them with the noninfluentials along a number of dimensions.

The influentials disproportionately represent those whose interests are immediately involved in the issue, as Table 9 strikingly demonstrates. Teachers (which here includes the school superintendent and the principals) comprise nearly half of the self-designated influentials. The results are even more striking when one considers that three of the farmers designated as influentials are school-board members and the two professionals are local ministers. In addition, of the five housewives, one is a minister's wife, another is a school-board member's wife,

14. Patterned after that employed in Katz and Lazarsfeld, *op. cit.*, pp. 346, 347.

two are wives of the superintendent and a principal, respectively, and another is the president of the locally powerful Woman's Christian Temperance Union. Thus a great proportion of those who designate themselves as influentials do occupy what we have referred to as strategic social location as far as this issue is concerned.

Additional features of the profile of the influential and how he compares with other respondents in Eastville-Westville are presented in Table 10. We see that most of the influentials are relative newcomers to the Eastville-Westville community. Whereas only 26 per cent of the respondents have lived in the community less than six years, nearly half of the self-designated opinion-leaders are included in this category. Nearly half of the respondents have lived in the community for over twenty years, while less than a third of the influentials have lived there that long. This obviously reflects the fact that teachers and school administrators make up such a large percentage of the influential classification. These people, by and large, were not native to the locale but came from elsewhere after receiving their preparatory training.

From these data, however, it is apparent that the influential is an active participant in the church life of the community, an important endeavor in Eastville-Westville. As a group, the influentials are more likely to be members of a church, they attend services to a significantly greater degree than others, and they participate to a slightly greater extent in those church activities beyond attendance. Religion to most of the influentials is more important than other of their activities, and it seemingly occupies as great a place in their value structure as in that of the noninfluential.

Congruent with the concept of opinion leadership, we find that the influentials reported being exposed to the issue to a greater extent through a variety of media, as Table 11 illustrates. Furthermore, opinion-leaders discussed the issue, informed others about it, and apprised officials of their feelings about it to a significantly greater extent than the noninfluentials. It is apparent that the influentials absorbed more information and that a greater variety of sources and channels of communication were open to them. Also they were able to discuss the issue with those in a position to act on the matter. Thus these self-designated influentials, in their daily activities and official responsibilities, were in a superior position for opinion leadership in this issue area.

Assuming that the influentials identified by the questionnaire re-

TABLE 10

Profile of Self-designated Influentials vis-à-vis Others in the Community

Dimension [a]	Category	Influentials		Others		Stat. Sig.
1. Time in community	1–6 years	47%		21%		
	6–20 years	22	(N = 36)	26	(N = 135)	$p < .01$
	Over 20 years	31		53		
5. Church membership	Yes	94%	(N = 36)	83%	(N = 136)	No
	No	6		17		
6. Church attendance	Once/wk or more	63%		55%		
	2–3 times/mo	26	(N = 35)	11	(N = 134)	$p < .02$
	Monthly or less	11		34		
7. Church participation	Very much	31%		23%		
	Average	44	(N = 36)	40	(N = 135)	No
	Minimal–none	25		37		
8. Importance of religion compared with other things	More	53%		53%		
	Same	28	(N = 36)	30	(N = 135)	No
	Less	19		17		
10–1. Knowledge of *Engel*	Correct	91%		66%		
	Don't know	6	(N = 34)	25	(N = 134)	$p < .02$
	Incorrect	3		9		
10–2. Knowledge of *Schempp*	Correct	82%		63%		
	Don't know	9	(N = 34)	26	(N = 134)	$p < .10$
	Incorrect	9		11		
15. Discussion with others	Yes	100%	(N = 35)	82%	(N = 131)	$p < .01$
	No	0		18		
17. Informed others of decisions	Yes	53%	(N = 36)	13%	(N = 132)	$p < .001$
	No	47		87		
25. Informed officials of feelings	Yes	68%	(N = 34)	14%	(N = 134)	$p < .001$
	No	32		86		

[a] Number preceding dimension indicates corresponding questionnaire item (see Appendix B).

TABLE 11

Sources Considered Most Helpful to Respondents
When Forming an Opinion on the Issue

Media	Influentials	Others
Mass media [a]	13 (38.2%)	70 (57.8%)
Religious communications [b]	2 (5.8)	9 (7.4)
Personal discussions	5 (14.7)	13 (10.7)
Combination [c]	14 (41.1%)	23 (19.0%)
	34 (99.8%)	115 (94.9%) [d]

[a] Includes newspapers, magazines, radio, and TV.
[b] Includes religious literature and ministers' sermons.
[c] When respondent indicated more than one source as being helpful, the combination category was indicated.
[d] Six others (4.9%) reported not recalling most important source.

sponse did in fact serve as the principal human channels through which the decisions were transmitted, what can one say about transmission adequacy? Once again examining Table 10, we see a significantly higher level of knowledge on the part of the influential as compared with the noninfluential. Not only do the influentials display greater knowledge of the recent *Engel* and *Schempp* rulings, but they also answered correctly more often the question pertaining to the *Zorach v. Clauson* case of over a decade ago.[15] Thus the principal human transmitters evidenced a relatively high level of knowledge.

As we noted before, however, influentials are not necessarily neutral transmitters of information; they convey values as well. It is thus important to examine their opinions about the relevant decisions and to ascertain their general attitudes toward the Court. Table 12 indicates that there is general disagreement with the Court's handling of the religion-in-public-school issue, although there is a significantly greater amount of agreement by the influentials than by others. To be sure, slightly over half of the influentials do not personally agree with the decisions.

Perhaps of more consequence are general attitudes toward the Court. It is understandable that all members of a society will not, on every occasion, agree with what its officials do. One may not like the

15. Forty-one per cent of the influentials correctly answered the question (item 10-3, Appendix B), 47 per cent incorrectly; of the noninfluentials, only 21 per cent answered this question correctly, while 37 per cent were incorrect. The differences were significant at the .01 level of probability.

TABLE 12

Agreement-Disagreement with Court Decisions Regarding Religious Practices in Public Schools

Item 27: "Do you agree or disagree with what the Court has said about religious practices in public schools?"

	Influentials		Others	
Agree	44%		22%	
Neutral	6	(N = 34)	24	(N = 135)
Disagree	50		54	

$\chi^2 = 14.6; p < .01$

Court's *Schempp* ruling while continuing to recognize the legitimacy of the Court to make such rulings. Thus, a series of questions was asked to elicit respondents' evaluations of the Court along a number of dimensions. The results of this line of questioning are contained in Table 13. The influentials disagree to a significantly greater extent than the noninfluentials that the justices decide cases on the bases of politics and special-interest orientation. They also disagree to a greater extent that the justices are pro-Communistic or that they show prefer-

TABLE 13

Comparison of Attitudes toward Court by Influentials and Others

Dimension [a]	Category	Influentials		Others		Stat. Sig.
28. Justices as politicians	Agree	15%		21%		
	Neutral	20	(N = 34)	39	(N = 134)	$p < .05$
	Disagree	65		40		
31. Justices as helping special interests	Agree	31%		28%		
	Neutral	22	(N = 36)	51	(N = 135)	$p < .01$
	Disagree	47		21		
32. Justices as pro-Communistic	Agree	14%		8%		
	Neutral	31	(N = 36)	61	(N = 133)	$p < .01$
	Disagree	55		31		
33. Court as pro-cities	Agree	14%		22%		
	Neutral	31	(N = 36)	51	(N = 136)	$p < .01$
	Disagree	55		27		

[a] Number preceding dimension indicates corresponding questionnaire item (see Appendix B).

ence to the city folk. To be sure, there is not much percentage difference between the influentials and noninfluentials who agree with these statements. It is striking, however, that so many noninfluentials have no opinion whatsoever on these matters, for these statements are quite damning as far as government and the administration of justice in this nation are concerned and evidence a considerable degree of alienation. But it is a cause for even greater concern that these statements did not elicit more disagreement from the influentials.

TABLE 14

Agreement-Disagreement with Desirability of Separation of Church and State as Far as Public Education Is Concerned

Item 39: "While I might think that religious practices in schoolrooms are good, in the long run the idea of 'separation of church and state' is beneficial to religion."

	Influentials		Others	
Agree	82%		55%	
Neutral	3	(N = 34)	14	(N = 124)
Disagree	15		31	

$\chi^2 = 8.6; p < .02$

Turning now to respondents' attitudes concerning various facets of the prayer decisions themselves (items 34 through 50, Appendix B), we may point to similar tendencies in responses. The desirability of the constitutional principle of "separation of church and state," for instance, is acknowledged by a significantly greater proportion of the influentials than by others (see Table 14). Nearly one-third of the noninfluentials disagree with this familiar societal norm when it is framed in operational terms, with only slightly over half of them agreeing with the statement. Similarly, Table 15 indicates that the majority of the noninfluential respondents perceive the Court's prayer decisions quite pessimistically. Fifty-six per cent of the noninfluentials perceive the Court's prayer decisions as contributing to an impending "Godless state" in America, compared with only 40 per cent of the influentials.

Thus there is a qualitative difference in perception of the Court and its decisions between the influentials and the noninfluentials. The latter group was less prone to dispute those statements which question the motives by which the Court decides issues. Similarly, noninfluen-

TABLE 15

Agreement-Disagreement That Decisions Are Step toward Godlessness

Item 46: "The real problem lies in this: these decisions are one more step toward making the U.S. a Godless state."

	Influentials	Others
Agree	40%	56%
Neutral	3 ($N = 35$)	10 ($N = 122$)
Disagree	57	34

$\chi^2 = 6.4; p < .05$

tials were more disposed to view the decisions superficially as enhancing godlessness. The noninfluential was significantly less attached to the principle of "separation of church and state" than the influential. These findings suggest that the influential evinces more affirmative attitudes toward the Court and its justices as part of the American political system and a greater acceptance of certain of the American "rules of the game." We would normally be hesitant to offer these results upon the limited evidence of this study; however, these findings are consistent with what other investigators have discovered. Samuel Stouffer, for instance, found, in a national survey, more tolerance and acceptance of democratic principles on the part of civic leaders than on the part of those less actively involved in public life.[16] Similar findings have been reported by Herbert McClosky from a national survey [17] and by Prothro and Grigg from a more limited comparative study.[18] To suggest that the influentials display a markedly more affirmative attitude toward the Court and its decisions than the noninfluentials does not appear to be off base.

In summary, the influentials in Eastville-Westville were those who, in their official capacity or interests, were in a position to know more about this issue and necessarily involved themselves with it more than others in the community. They discussed the issue and informed others to a significantly greater extent than those who did not designate themselves as influentials. Not only did the bulk of the self-styled

16. *Communism, Conformity and Civil Liberties* (New York: Doubleday & Co., Inc., 1955).

17. "Consensus and Ideology in American Politics," 58 *American Political Science Review* 361 (1964).

18. James W. Prothro and C. W. Grigg, "Fundamental Principles of Democracy: Bases of Agreement and Disagreement," 22 *Journal of Politics* 276 (1960).

influentials have connections in the communications networks of the public school apparatus, but they also were for the most part quite active participants in the religious life of the community. This latter aspect of Eastville-Westville is very important, as the next chapter will illustrate. These church contacts with the less active segments of the population afforded the influentials an opportunity to convey information as well as related values. Thus, the influentials may have performed a temporizing function in the community which contributed to the relative calm with which this locality reacted to the Court's prayer decisions.

CHAPTER 9

The Dynamics of Response

In our earlier discussion we noted that an individual may or may not agree privately with a ruling while recognizing a public duty of compliance. In Eastville-Westville a large number of persons personally disagreed with the policy but felt that it must nevertheless be complied with. On the other hand, a number of people went so far as to deny that a public obligation of compliance existed. It is obvious, then, that individuals may respond to Supreme Court policy in a number of ways. An examination of these dimensions of private acceptance and public compliance and their possible combinations allows us to understand more fully the dynamics of compliance at the local level.

We may combine the notions of private acceptance and public compliance in various ways to produce what shall hereafter be referred to as "modes of response." If indices of these dimensions are based on a three-point scale (agree-neutral-disagree), nine distinct modes of response are theoretically possible, ranging from that in which private acceptance is combined with a recognition of the obligation to publicly comply to one in which neither private acceptance nor public compliance is recognized. A summary of the derivation of the various modes of response and the number of respondents empirically found in each category is contained in Table 16. Only seven of the nine possible combinations were found empirically. These modes of response, as indicated in Table 16, are given letter designations from A to G. An individual in agreement with both indices would be classified as a Mode A respondent. Mode E contains those who acknowledge the duty to comply with the ruling but do not privately agree with the policy. Those who combine private disagreement with the rulings and

TABLE 16

Basic Modes of Response to Court Interpretation and Respective Frequencies

Public Compliance [a]	Private Acceptance [b]		
	Agree	Neutral	Disagree
Agree	A (39)	C (16)	E (30)
Neutral		G (5)	
Disagree	B (4)	D (11)	F (54)

[a] *Public Compliance:* "No matter what one may think about religious practices, if the Supreme Court says they are unconstitutional, one has the duty to accept the decision and act accordingly."

[b] *Private Acceptance:* "Do you agree or disagree with what the Court has said about religious practices in public schools?"

rejection of a public duty of compliance are found in Mode F, and so forth. In the ensuing discussion the mode-of-response categories will be referred to merely in terms of their letter designations.

Using these modes of response, we may now observe more precisely how important elements of the social system reacted to the Court's determinations. We see, for instance, that many important actors are included among the Mode A respondents. The superintendent is found there along with three of the four school principals. The only principal not found in Mode A is the assistant principal of the junior high school—a school virtually unaffected by the implementation of the Court's policy. More teachers are likewise found in Mode A than in any other category, while the same is true for community influentials. Two school-board members are similarly Mode A respondents. It is clear, then, that major elements of the Eastville-Westville school district personally felt that the course taken by the Supreme Court with regard to prayers in the public schools was right and consequently felt that the rulings should be obeyed in their locale. Furthermore, Table 17 indicates that most of the remaining occupants of special systemic roles were found in those modes of response which entailed recognition of the obligation to comply.

From this analysis, it becomes more clear how a new superintendent of schools could come into this highly traditional religious community

TABLE 17

Composition of Mode-of-Response Categories

Roles	Modes of Response						
	A	B	C	D	E	F	G
Community totals	39	4	16	11	30	54	5
Superintendent	1						
Former superintendent					1		
School board	2		2		1	2	
Principals	3					1	
Teachers	11				6	7	
Influentials	13	2	2	1	6	10	

and upset a desired custom without incurring the wrath of the community. Regardless of their personal feelings in the matter, many persons recognized a public obligation to bring their local practices into perceived congruence with Court policy. Of more importance was the distribution of such attitudes. Extensive support for compliance already existed among important actors in the system, many of whom personally recognized the desirability of the policy enunciated by the Court. This body of support lay dormant but performed an important function when tapped by the new superintendent. Forces which already existed were mobilized to support compliance with the Court's rulings.

• Factors of Response

As we have seen, individuals responded to the Court's prayer decisions in a variety of ways. How can we account for these differences in the mode of response? What factors appear to be relevant as individuals adopt differing postures toward the Court and implementation of its policies? The theory presented earlier should be instructive as we attempt to grapple with these questions.

To recapitulate, the theory presented in Chapter 2 suggests that compliance with Supreme Court determinations lies partially in the variety of power relationships existing between the Court and those affected by its rulings. That is to say, the Court has the ability to move individuals in desired directions by "tapping" certain bases of power. The bases suggested as most apropos for Supreme Court decision-making were referred to as *coercive, legitimate,* and *expert* power. The dynamics of this decision-making process involve the notion of "cognitive balance." That is, when knowledge of Supreme Court rulings is considered in proximity to knowledge of social processes which run counter to the rulings, an imbalanced psychological structure ensues with concomitant normal pressures to return the organism to a balanced state. This balance may be restored by altering overt behavior to make it congruent with the Court's policy. Thus, various role-players may attempt to bring practices under their jurisdiction into perceived compliance with a Court ruling, not necessarily because of direct legal necessity but rather because they recognize the expertise or the legitimacy of the Court.

This sort of imbalance may be removed in other ways than changing overt behavior; as we have seen, it may be attacked purely on the cognitive level. A number of ways in which this may be accomplished were discussed in Chapter 2. Ongoing practices may be *differentiated* from those banned by the Court. The Court itself or its rulings may be attacked to justify noncompliance, a process referred to as *denial.* Various positive factors may be associated with the proscribed practice to *bolster* it and help "drown out" imbalance. Finally, an elaborate *transcendent* structure may be constructed to justify noncompliance and restore cognitive balance.

This theory, embodying bases for either acceptance or rejection of Court policy, was translated into a series of questionnaire items.[1] An examination of these items indicates that nearly every facet of the theory was tapped. A summary of these items listed by their major themes and the respective response percentages is contained in Table 18. We see, for instance, that various aspects of legitimate power were put into operational form, e.g., item 38, charisma; item 39, legalistic authority; item 47, traditional authority; and item 49, "internalization." Coercive power and expert power served as bases for other questions. Also, based upon the theory of cognitive balance, a number of items were devised embodying justification for noncompliance with the Court's rulings. Item 44, for example, embodies the notion of "differentiation," where it is suggested that classroom prayers conducted by the teacher on her own may be differentiated from those programs held unconstitutional by the Court. Item 48 suggests that the prayer rulings are elements in a more extensive trend in this nation

1. See Appendix B, items 34 through 50. For a brief discussion of interview and questionnaire procedures utilized in this study see Appendix A, "Methodological Considerations."

TABLE 18

Response to Questionnaire Items Tapping Bases of Acceptance or Rejection of Supreme Court Policy

Item	Theme [a]	Agree	Disagree	No Opinion
34.	Public compliance—Legitimacy	50.0%	40.9%	9.1%
35.	*Denial*—Exceeded power range	71.0	19.3	9.7
36.	Coercive power of Court	34.1	52.3	13.6
37.	*Denial*—Local responsibility	51.7	35.2	13.1
38.	Legitimate power—Charisma	43.2	37.5	19.3
39.	Legitimate power—Legalistic	55.7	25.6	18.8
40.	*Denial*—Aid negative ref. groups	58.5	19.3	22.2
41.	Coercive power of Court	47.2	30.1	22.7
42.	*Bolstering*—Community desires	38.1	48.3	13.7
43.	*Bolstering*—Child benefit	40.3	36.4	23.3
44.	*Differentiation*—Teacher responsibility	51.1	29.5	19.3
45.	Expert power of Court	69.9	11.9	18.2
46.	*Denial*—Step toward godless state	48.3	35.2	16.5
47.	Legitimate power—Tradition	49.4	33.5	17.0
48.	*Transcendence*—Fits godless pattern	53.4	31.8	14.8
49.	Legitimate power—Internalization	34.1	38.6	27.3
50.	Legitimate power—Citizen duty	57.4	32.4	10.2

[a] For precise wording see Appendix B.

toward crime, divorce, delinquency, etc. This item was devised to tap the notion of "transcendence." The themes listed in Table 18 may be cross-checked with the precise wording used in the questionnaire (Appendix B) for further examples of this attempt at operationalization of the concepts.

The theory presented in Chapter 2, then, pointed to the sorts of questions which should be asked to ascertain why people accept or reject Supreme Court interpretation. The patterns by which individuals responded to these questions will help explain the differences in the modes of response discussed earlier.

From the responses to the seventeen items presented in Table 18 a smaller number of clearly identifiable factors emerged which are theoretically valid and more readily usable for analytical purposes. The mathematical technique of factor analysis was used to abstract the factors described below. This technique is based on the notion that, given a number of interrelated indices or variables, "interrelationships may be due to the presence of one or more underlying variables or *factors* which are related to the indices to varying degrees." [2] The nature of the factors extracted may be determined by analyzing what the indices most highly correlated with the factor have in common.

The outcome of the factor analysis of the seventeen items is con-

TABLE 19

Rotated Factor Matrix

	Factor			
Item	1	2	3	4
34	– *.5723*	– .1289	.3733	.3623
35	.3760	*.5259*	– .2680	.1833
36	– .1770	– .0833	.1945	*.7060*
37	*.6876*	.2801	– .1466	.0814
38	.0991	.0480	.0645	*.7239*
39	– .0628	– .1586	*.5989*	– .0179
40	.1247	*.7497*	– .0453	– .0143
41	– *.4194*	.1965	.3900	.3738
42	*.7546*	.1745	– .1892	– .0499
43	*.7283*	.2510	– .1877	.0231
44	*.5420*	.3805	.1732	– .3575
45	– .0193	.0131	.1740	*.6792*
46	.2484	*.8115*	– .2124	– .0177
47	– .2023	– .0766	*.7015*	.4139
48	.2263	*.7992*	– .2654	– .0624
49	– .2004	– .2955	*.6481*	.1670
50	– .1910	– .1379	*.6784*	.2780

tained in Table 19.[3] Each item was correlated with every other item, and factors were extracted according to the degree to which they explained the variation among the indices. In this case, the variance was explained through the extraction of four factors. Each item is correlated with each factor to varying degrees; the correlation between the item and the factor is referred to as the "factor loading." In Table

2. Hubert M. Blalock, Jr., *Social Statistics* (New York: McGraw-Hill Book Co., Inc., 1960), p. 383; Chapter 21, "Factor Analysis and Other Multivariate Techniques," presents a brief but clear explanation of this technique. A much more detailed account may be found in Benjamin Fruchter, *Introduction to Factor Analysis* (Princeton: D. Van Nostrand Co., Inc., 1954).

3. For this analysis the Centroid Factor Analysis program and Varimax Factor Rotation program for an IBM 7090 computer were used. Both programs were supplied by the Statistical Services Unit of the University of Illinois.

19 the largest factor loading for each index is set in italics to indicate the factor with which the item is most highly correlated. For instance, item 34 is most highly correlated, although negatively, with factor 1, while item 35 is most highly correlated with factor 2, and so forth. Let us interpret the factors by considering the items most highly correlated with each one of them.

The first factor, as Table 20 indicates, is related to the notion of

TABLE 20

Factor 1—Local Responsibility

Item		Factor Loading
34.	No matter what one may think about religious practices, if the Supreme Court says they are unconstitutional, one has the duty to accept the decision and act accordingly.	– *.5723*
37.	Since local officials are responsible for what goes on in the schools, they should decide whether or not to have prayers and Bible readings and not some far-off court.	*.6876*
41.	No matter what local school officials think, they must do what the Court says to prevent the federal government from moving in and using force.	– *.4194*
42.	Our school officials should do what the people of the community want rather than what the Supreme Court says that we should want.	*.7546*
43.	The positive good for the child connected with religion in the schools more than offsets knowing that you are not doing exactly as the Supreme Court has said.	*.7283*
44.	While the Court may say that school boards may not require classroom prayers, there is no reason why teachers can't allow them on their own.	*.5420*

"local responsibility" insofar as religious exercises in the public schools are concerned. The items positively correlated with this factor all express the sentiment that actors associated with the local educational system should be the ones to determine whether or not such practices should take place: local school officials should decide; the wishes of the community should be considered; local teachers are really not precluded from having prayers in their own classrooms; the benefits derived by the children from religious exercises in school outweigh such less immediate and indirect concerns as compliance with the orders of a remote court.

Two items, 34 and 41, are negatively correlated with this factor. Upon inspection, it is readily apparent that both express the idea of national action. No matter what is thought locally, there must be compliance with the Court's policy or else force by the federal government may be used to bring about compliant behavior. Since these items so obviously involve a national rather than a local responsibility, it is understandable why they correlate negatively with this factor.

The notion of local responsibility or local legitimacy may be utilized by individuals to justify noncompliance with the Court's policy, and

TABLE 21

Factor 2—Rewards to Negative Reference Groups

Item		Factor Loading
35.	Although the Court should interpret the Constitution, it has gone too far when it starts telling us that we can't pray in our schools.	*.5259*
40.	The problem with these decisions is that they aid undesirable Godless groups.	*.7497*
46.	The real problem lies in this: these decisions are one more step toward making the U.S. a Godless state.	*.8115*
48.	These decisions may seem harmless, but they fit into the general trend in this country toward Godlessness, corruption, crime, divorce, and delinquency.	*.7992*

the various mechanisms discussed earlier—denial, bolstering, and differentiation—may serve to restore cognitive balance. An imbalanced state results from a recognition that religious practices in the schools run counter to what the Supreme Court has said on this matter. Balance may result, not through overt behavioral change in this case, but by handling the problem cognitively. The problem may be viewed as one which is properly dealt with on the local level rather than by a remote national body. It is a local affair to be handled locally; thus behavioral change in light of the Supreme Court's ruling need not take place.

The second factor, reported in Table 21, pertains to the notion that the Supreme Court's *Engel* and *Schempp* rulings in substance constitute rewards to negative reference groups. Not only do the rulings reward individuals and groups who hold views patently alien to one's own, but they are actually a part of the fearful trend in this nation toward secularism and its attendant evils.

Although the reason may not be evident on the surface, it does make sense that item 35 is included in factor 2. This item, which is expressive of the notion of range of power, was frequently brought up during interviews. In many instances the Court itself was not attacked for the rulings which the interviewees may have feared and detested; what drew their ire was rather the groups which had brought the cases into Court. Some said that the Supreme Court had no business dealing with such matters, although they could conceive of no "out" for the Court when it is presented with such controversies. Hence there was for some interviewees a direct relationship between these negative reference groups and the notion that the Court had exceeded its proper range of power.

This element seemed to be particularly important in Eastville-Westville, as numerous interviewees complained of the rulings in these terms. The president of the school board was explicit on this point. He saw the outcome of the cases as a product of the conspiracy of the anti-Christ forces that are slowly devouring American society. Getting prayers out of the school was only one step in the process; "In God We Trust" would surely come off our coins, and references to the Almighty would be stricken from our national documents and from the pledge of allegiance.

Perception of the rulings as expressive of aid to negative reference groups once again allows the individual to justify nonacceptance and noncompliance. Behavioral change in the direction of compliance is not necessary to establish cognitive balance, as this may again be accomplished solely at the cognitive level. That is, the decisions and the Court itself may be attacked directly through the mechanism of denial, or a transcendent structure may be devised to restore cognitive balance.

The third factor is designated the "national legitimacy" factor. It is obvious from an examination of Table 22 that each of the items most highly correlated with this factor involves an aspect of legitimate power associated with national authorities. We see, for instance, an index of "traditional authority" (47) as well as one involving "legal authority" (39). Both indexes are acknowledged as a base of legitimacy in the Weberian formulation. Item 49 expresses the idea of "internalization"—acceptance because it conforms to one's personal values—a component which has a basis in modern social psychological theory and research.[4] The final item, 50, connotes a more general notion of

4. Herbert C. Kelman, "Compliance, Identification and Internalization: Three Processes of Attitude Change," 2 *Journal of Conflict Resolution* 51 (1958).

TABLE 22

Factor 3—National Legitimacy

Item		Factor Loading
39.	While I might think that religious practices in schoolrooms are good, in the long run the idea of "separation of church and state" is beneficial to religion.	*.5989*
47.	Although we may disagree, we must accept what the Court has said, since it has traditionally had the job of telling us what the Constitution means.	*.7015*
49.	I support these decisions because they express the true meaning of constitutional church-state separation.	*.6481*
50.	While one may dislike what the Court says at times, one must accept its decisions to be a good citizen.	*.6784*

acceptance of Supreme Court interpretation as one of a number of obligations an individual has to the political system of which he is a member. All of these aspects were mentioned in Chapter 2 as bases of legitimate power. Their interrelationship in this factor suggests that they do in fact tap the same basic notion.

Legitimacy, as previously noted, is an important basis for Supreme Court power. When the Supreme Court has made a ruling in accordance with the widely accepted Constitution, individuals in a variety of roles are motivated to accept and comply regardless of their personal feelings about the matter in question. The Court, by tradition and legal prescription, is the appropriate body for making such determinations, and public compliance is perceived to be the proper response.

The final factor is involved with the notion of expertise. As shown in Table 23, item 45 clearly refers to the expertise of the justices which

TABLE 23

Factor 4—Expertise

Item		Factor Loading
36.	Even though we may want to continue our local practices, we can't fight the power of the federal courts.	*.7060*
38.	Supreme Court judges have the natural abilities to tell us what the Constitution really means.	*.7239*
45.	The Constitution is a mighty complicated thing, so it's fortunate that we have a body of well-trained judges to tell us what it means.	*.6792*

accrues from their specialized training. Item 38, dealing with the "natural abilities" of the justices to interpret the Constitution properly, was inspired originally by the Weberian notion of "charisma." According to his formulation, this was one basis for legitimate power. We find in our analysis, however, that this item correlated very weakly with the legitimacy factor (see Table 19) but much more so with the expertise factor. The item as worded clearly entails a personal ability of a quite specialized nature.

The one item which at first glance does not seem similar to the others that are highly correlated with this factor is item 36. This item was originally included in the instrument to tap the notion of coercive power, but further reflection makes its inclusion in the expertise factor theoretically tenable. As discussed in the early chapters, the workings of the Court system in general are beyond the experience and comprehension of most people. When a conflict reaches the judiciary for resolution, it enters an arena where the usual rules of the political game do not hold, and it is ultimately the Court which has the special ability to say whether or not a practice conforms to the Constitution. In this sense item 36 is congruent with the others more directly expressive of the expertise notion.

Expertise, as well as legitimacy, is an important basis of power which the Court may tap to motivate compliant behavior on the part of individuals. No matter what an individual may think privately, if this expert group of legal authorities says that the Constitution precludes prayer in elementary schools, then individuals have no choice but to accept its judgment and act accordingly.

The seventeen items were thus reduced to four clear-cut and theoretically significant factors through factor-analytic procedures. It should be emphasized, however, that the resulting factors assume importance only insofar as they are useful in understanding the dynamics of response to the Court's decisions in Eastville-Westville. That is, do these factors help us to understand why community conflict did not follow the decision to halt the lunch-time prayers? We contend that these factors are quite useful in this regard. They are useful, first of all, in explaining the differing modes of response found in the community and, second, in understanding the actions of significant role occupants in the community.

Each respondent was given a score on each factor by summing his responses to those items which were most highly correlated with each factor. For convenience in comparison, the three indices having the largest factor loadings were used to determine the individual factor scores. Inspection of Table 19 shows that each factor includes three items which have roughly equivalent factor loadings and which have significantly higher loadings than the remaining items. The factor score, then, is the total score a respondent has received for the three items in each factor. Since the respondent could indicate agreement or disagreement with the statement in terms of a seven-point scale—"1" indicating strong agreement and "7" indicating strong disagreement—factor scores based on the three indices may therefore range from 3 to 21, the lower scores indicating agreement with the direction of the factor, with 12 as the neutral position. Since the respondents had previously been categorized into seven modes of response (see Table 16), their scores on the respective factors could be summed and four mean factor scores derived for each of the modes.

If there is any validity at all to the factors that have been extracted, one should find significant differences between the mean factor scores of the various modes of response. For instance, one should find significantly higher mean scores on factor 1 (local responsibility) and factor 2 (negative reference groups) in Mode A, which entails both private acceptance and the duty of public compliance, than in Mode F, which entails neither. The reverse situation would be expected when comparing these modes as to their mean scores on factor 3 (national legitimacy) and factor 4 (expertise). Of most importance are the differences in mean factor scores between Modes E and F respondents, both of which privately disagree with the rulings but differ as to an acknowledgment of the necessity for public compliance.

The modes of response with their respective mean factor scores are summarized in Table 24. Because there is clear-cut agreement or disagreement as far as private acceptance and public compliance are concerned, we shall focus our analysis primarily upon Modes A, E, and F.[5] We see that Mode A has by far the largest mean factor scores on

5. Mode B is also clear-cut on these dimensions, although it seems to be a spurious category. It is difficult to imagine an individual privately agreeing with a policy while rejecting the notion of public compliance. Three of the four respondents in this category were interviewed; one is the wife of a school-board member, another is the pastor of the Westville church, and the third is a reputed "influential," a Westville businessman. An examination of the completed questionnaires shows the latter two respondents indicating a qualified position as far as private acceptance is concerned. The returned questionnaire of the fourth respondent in this category reveals that, while he "strongly agrees" with the Supreme Court rulings, his knowledge scores on the relevant decisions indicates a total lack of awareness of what the Court had said. Consequently, it must be concluded that this is not a valid category.

TABLE 24

Modes of Response to Court Policy, with Respective Mean Factor Scores

	Factor			
	1	2	3	4
Modes of Response [a]	Local Responsibility	Rewards to Negative Reference Groups	National Legitimacy	Expertise
A. Public and private compliance (N = 39)	16.3 [b]	15.4	7.8	9.8
B. Private only, not public (N = 4)	14.5	14.3	14.5	15.8
C. Public compliance (private?) (N = 16)	11.8	10.5	8.4	7.1
D. No public (private?) (N = 11)	9.5	9.9	14.0	13.3
E. Public but not private (N = 30)	12.1	8.7	10.3	11.0
F. Neither public nor private (N = 54)	8.4	7.6	14.0	12.3

[a] Since Mode G, which contains respondents who are completely indifferent on both the private-acceptance and public-compliance dimensions, is of minor significance both theoretically and numerically, it is not included in this analysis.

[b] Scores may range from 3 to 21, with low scores indicating agreement. The midpoint or neutral position is 12.

factors 1 and 2 while having the lowest scores on factors 3 and 4. This is understandable. Since the respondents in this category privately agree with what the Court has said about religious practices in public schools, one would expect them to disagree that this is a matter to be handled locally or that the rulings penalize godliness. By the same token, it is not surprising to find these respondents also acknowledging to a greater extent the legitimate and expert bases of Court power.

Viewing the mean factor scores in Mode E—those who disagree privately but acknowledge a public responsibility for compliance—we see that the largest mean score is associated with factor 2. Respondents agree that the Court's rulings are rewarding to negative reference groups. On the local-responsibility factor the mean score indicates an indifference, as the score stands on dead center. On both the legitimacy and expertise factors the Mode E mean scores indicate a tendency in the direction of agreement.

As opposed to this, the mean factor scores in Mode F—the "neither private acceptance nor public compliance" category—indicate strong agreement among respondents on factors 1 and 2, with disagreement and neutrality on the legitimacy and expertise factors, respectively. That is to say, the Mode F respondents tend to believe that the problem of religious activities in the public schools is properly one of local not national concern and that the Court rulings in this matter have rewarded godless groups. These respondents tend to disagree with the legitimacy of the Court in this area and are largely indifferent to the notion that the Court possesses the expertise to make the proper judgments in this as well as other areas.

TABLE 25

Statistical Comparison between Mean Factor Scores among Pairs of Modes of Response

	Factors							
Difference of Means	1		2		3		4	
between Modes:	*t*	*p*	*t*	*p*	*t*	*p*	*t*	*p*
A and E	4.12	.001	5.26	.001	2.48	.02	1.05	n.s.
E and F	3.49	.001	.97	n.s.	3.62	.001	1.29	n.s.

$$t = \frac{\bar{X}_1 - \bar{X}_2}{\hat{\sigma}(\bar{x}_1 - \bar{x}_2)} \text{ where } \hat{\sigma}(\bar{x}_1 - \bar{x}_2) = \sqrt{\left(\frac{s_1^2}{N_1 - 1}\right) + \left(\frac{s_2^2}{N_2 - 1}\right)}$$

In a statistical sense, are the mean factor scores significantly different among the three modes of response which we are investigating? To answer this question, a series of difference-of-means tests was conducted to compare the means of the four factors between Modes A and E which differ only on the public-compliance dimension. The results are summarized in Table 25, where it will be noted that the mean factor scores in Modes A and E differ significantly on all factors except factor 4, the expertise factor. Even on the legitimacy factor, which is concurred in by both categories, the respondents in Mode A acknowledge this basis to a significantly greater degree than those in Mode E, even though the latter generally recognize this basis. This is not the case with expertise, however, as both groups acknowledge this factor to a comparable extent.

A comparison of factor means between respondents of Modes E and F reveals that the two groups do not differ significantly on two of the factors. To a comparable extent, both tend to feel rather strongly that the rulings of the Court reward the forces of godlessness in this country. In this regard both groups differ significantly from the private accepters of Mode A. This could reflect a deeper religious commitment on the part of Mode E and F respondents than those in Mode A, and a comparison of the groups on a "religiosity" factor shows that this is the case.[6] Modes E and F, as Table 26 illustrates, had mean factor scores

TABLE 26

Modes of Response Compared as to Religiosity-Factor Means

Response Modes	Religiosity-Factor Means	
A	10.67 [a]	$t = 3.69$
E	6.47	$p = < .001$
F	6.65	

[a] Since four items were included in this factor, scores may range from 4 to 28, with low scores indicating a strong religiosity. The midpoint or neutral position is 16.

lower than the mean factor score of Mode A, a difference significant at the .001 level.

Of both statistical and theoretical significance are the differences between these groups with respect to factors 1 and 3. Table 24 indicates that those who acknowledge the duty of public compliance, Mode E, are completely indifferent to the notion that matters involving religious practices in the schools should be left to the locality, while those who reject public compliance agree with this notion quite strongly. The difference in the mean response between the two

6. This factor was extracted from a factor analysis of the group of varied attitudinal questions (items 51 through 82). See Appendix B. The items having the greatest factor loadings—hence used to derive the factor scores—are items 55, 60, 65, and 77. Items 55, 60, and 77 were originally obtained from a scale of "religious conventionalism" contained in E. Francesco, "A Pervasive Value: Conventional Religiosity," 57 *Journal of Social Psychology* 467 (1962). Item 65 is from the "authoritarianism" subscale of Rokeach's "Dogmatism" scale in his *Open and Closed Mind* (New York: Basic Books, Inc., 1960), p. 77. Other factors extracted from items 51 through 82 were identifiable as pertaining to economic and political liberalism-conservatism, faith in people, and local *vs.* cosmopolitan values. Only on the religiosity factor does one find significant differences in mean factor scores between Modes A, E, and F.

categories is statistically significant at the .001 level, as indicated in Table 25. On factor 3, national legitimacy, we find the public compliers, Mode E, agreeing and those who reject public compliance, Mode F, disagreeing, the difference in mean score again being significant at the .001 level. The Mode E respondents do not like what the Court has said, but the legitimacy of the Court is a reality for them, offsetting whatever private sentiments they may hold. The Mode F respondents, on the other hand, think the rulings reward repugnant interests and also feel very strongly that religion in public schools is a matter to be dealt with on the local level rather than by the national court system. Recognition of a local legitimacy in the matter entails a rejection of the legitimacy basis of the national Supreme Court. This can also be observed in Mode D—those who are privately indifferent but who reject the necessity for public compliance. These respondents similarly acknowledge the local-responsibility notion embodied in factor 1 while rejecting the legitimacy basis in factor 3.

Furthermore, it may be suggested that what Lipset has called the "superimposition of cleavages" [7] is operative as far as the Mode F respondents are concerned. That is to say, the religious cleavage implied in factor 2 is actually reinforced by the notion of local legitimacy embodied in factor 1. While we do not have questionnaire data directly bearing on this point, the impression received by the author in interviews in the community strongly suggests such superimposition. In our discussion of the church life of Eastville-Westville in Chapter 7 we noted that the ministers of the dominant Methodist churches were reportedly in difficulty in their respective churches. In the view of some parishioners they expressed ideas alien to the Fundamentalism of the *local* church. The denominational hierarchy was likewise viewed by some as being suspect. In Eastville or Westville it is the local church that is important; the denominational ties of the church are secondary.

An analysis of mean factor scores among the various mode-of-response categories therefore indicates that those who personally agree with the substance of Supreme Court policy also acknowledge to a greater extent the Court's legitimacy and expert bases than do those who are displeased with the substantive ruling. This is not an earth-shattering finding, to be sure. Among those who find the rulings repugnant to religious values, whether or not a responsibility for public compliance is recognized hinges primarily on the notion of

7. Seymour M. Lipset, *Political Man* (Garden City: Doubleday & Co., Inc., 1959).

legitimacy. Some people who do not privately accept the rulings nevertheless acknowledge the legitimacy which surrounds the Court. These individuals—the Mode E respondents—recognize the duty of public compliance because the Supreme Court is, for one reason or another, considered to be an appropriate body for making such determinations. In this instance it may be said that the Court has tapped the legitimacy basis of power to obtain compliance with its ruling.

Mode F respondents, whose religious sensibilities have been offended to no greater extent than the Mode E respondents, do not similarly recognize the duty of public compliance. The legitimacy of the Court cannot be involved here because the Mode F respondents feel strongly that the matter must be handled on the local level—by local school officials and teachers. Psychological imbalance caused by a knowledge that local practices are not in accord with what the Court has said, then, can be redressed by the various mechanisms discussed earlier (differentiation, denial, and bolstering).

Finally, Table 27 shows the distribution of factor scores among the main actors in the Eastville-Westville school system. The superintendent, whose action was crucial in the implementation of Court policy in the system, scores the maximum amount on factors 1 and 2, indicating complete disagreement with the underlying notions that local responsibility is paramount and that the decisions have rewarded godless groups. Factor 2 discloses the largest difference between the superintendent and his predecessor, who indicated strong belief that the rulings have rewarded the forces of the godless. Among the school-board members (numbers 6 through 12 in Table 27) we observe a considerable range of scores on each factor. Particularly noteworthy is the fact that member "A," the current president of the school board, who revealed himself in the interview as a man of deep and fundamental religious convictions, is the member with the most extreme scores. On the first two factors he scores nearly perfect agreement, while on the last two factors he definitely tends toward disagreement. It should be noted his views differ significantly from the majority of his board. The school principals approach the superintendent in their denial of factors 1 and 2. The legitimacy factor draws most agreement from the principals, while the two elementary-school principals disagree rather vigorously with the expertise dimension.

If we compare the superintendent's position on these four factors with the mean response of the total sample, the "influentials," and the school board, it becomes clear that the superintendent does not stand

TABLE 27

Factor Scores of System Actors

Actor	Factors 1: Local Responsibility	2: Rewards to Negative Reference Groups	3: Legitimacy	4: Expertise
1. Sample mean	11.5 [a]	10.4	11.2	11.1
2. Influential mean	12.8	12.5	11.4	12.3
3. Superintendent	21.0	21.0	5.0	9.0
4. Former superintendent	13.0	3.0	9.0	8.0
5. School-board mean	10.7	11.1	8.9	8.0
6. School-board member A	3.0	4.0	15.0	15.0
7. School-board member B	6.0	6.0	11.0	10.0
8. School-board member C	19.0	16.0	5.0	5.0
9. School-board member D	11.0	11.0	5.0	7.0
10. School-board member E	16.0	12.0	5.0	3.0
11. School-board member F	5.0	15.0	15.0	10.0
12. School-board member G	15.0	14.0	6.0	6.0
13. Eastville principal	21.0	21.0	7.0	17.0
14. Westville principal	14.0	20.0	13.0	15.0
15. High-school principal	21.0	21.0	3.0	4.0

[a] Scores may range from 3 to 21, with low scores indicating agreement with the direction of the factor, high scores indicating disagreement. The midpoint or neutral position is 12.

in the "mainstream" of the community. The former superintendent is much closer to the modal response of the community and to its "influentials" and its elected school board than is the present incumbent.

• *Summary*

The Supreme Court's policy concerning religious practices in public schools ran counter to the prevailing values in the Eastville-Westville district. Nevertheless, the central decision-maker for the school system found the policy congruent with his privately held notions and brought the system into a state of compliance with the rulings. Instead of arousing a great deal of controversy, the action was generally supported or at least accepted with good grace. A deeper study of response to the Court's rulings indicates that there were compelling factors which offset private disagreement with the substance of the Court's policy. The legitimacy of the Court and its expertise are examples of such offsetting factors. Thus some individuals felt that the ruling was an aid to groups they deplore, yet they grudgingly acknowledged their duty to do what the Court said because it is the appropriate body for making such determinations or because it possesses the necessary skills to discover what the Constitution "really means" in the "establishment of religion" clause of the First Amendment. On the other hand, others stubbornly disavowed a duty to comply with the Court's rulings and countered a notion of national legitimacy with one of local legitimacy. In Eastville-Westville, however, those acknowledging a duty to comply with the rulings were in the majority, particularly so in the case of the community influentials, the school board, and the educational staff. Consequently, the superintendent had a rather firm basis of support for the action he took.

CHAPTER 10

Conclusion

SUPREME COURT DECISION-MAKING has now been seen on a very comprehensive scale, and a summation is in order. The thesis which has been maintained throughout is that this particular decision-making process entails behavior on the part of numerous actors in the political system. Activity on the part of the Court as the source of the verbal messages obviously is involved, but since "decision" entails *effective* determination of policy, it is mandatory that a variety of actors participate. Some individuals function as channels through which the Court's policies are transmitted to the level of implementation, while others at this level act to transform the messages into behavior congruent with the Court's determination. Only through the coordinated actions of all of these actors is the decision-making process consummated.

It is useful to restate the dynamics of this process as hypothesized in the early chapters. Behavior consistent with Supreme Court rulings results from a variety of power relationships built upon certain underlying bases. That is to say, compliant behavior follows the enunciation of Court policy because individuals who are in positions to give substance to such policy are influenced by the legitimacy surrounding the Court, the expertise of the justices, and/or elements of coercion. They then seek to bring practices under their jurisdiction into perceived congruence with the Court's determination. Presumably their action is ratified by others less actively involved in policy-making yet directly affected by the policy, once again because of the existence of these underlying power bases.

In order that one or more of these types of relationships may be invoked, we have observed that the Court itself possesses certain important resources. The judiciary, as part of the political system, shares in the general coercive powers associated with government. As we have noted, however, the sanctions immediately available to the Court itself are minimal and may be applied in a narrowly circumscribed set of instances. The legitimate and expertise bases are much more pervasive elements of this decision-making system. Constitutional arrangements have set the Court apart from the other components of the political system and have specified that it is the proper body for handling certain kinds of conflict through rather well-defined and esoteric modes of procedure. Beyond this, the Court is traditionally staffed by specially trained individuals who carry out their business in a manner conducive to the acceptance of their rulings. The impression engendered by the Court—the image it presents to its immediate or distant audiences—is one of majestic fairness, reasonableness, and expertness.

To reach the broadest possible audience, the Court through its verbal messages also provides incentives for acceptance of its policies. Persuasive arguments are presented, allusions to the miranda of the political system are made, and impressions are engendered that the Court is an expert body through the frequent citation of precedents and other esoteric manifestations of the law. Thus, through institutional arrangements, patterns of recruitment, and modes of behavior the Supreme Court is able to invoke the legitimacy and expertise relationships which result in compliant behavior on the part of those who are under obligation to act.

The crucial stage is, of course, at the level of implementation. Unless action congruent with the Court's ruling is carried out at this point, there cannot be a fully effective decision. To study the dynamics of the process at this level, we investigated what happened in the Eastville-Westville School District as a result of the Court's rulings regarding religious practices in the public schools. In order to get a full picture of the workings of the system, we must closely consider the material presented in Chapters 7, 8, and 9, which shows that the compliance process is a mix of psychological and social factors.

Whether or not Supreme Court policy is implemented depends on whether the policy is relevant to the situation obtaining in the community and whether key actors in the social system are aware of the relationships between the rulings and the ongoing social processes. In Eastville-Westville these conditions held. The central decision-maker for the relevant social system—the district school superintendent—was quite aware of the Court's policy; he strongly agreed with it and perceived that exercises in the schools under his jurisdiction ran counter to it. Action was taken; practices in the schools were altered to bring them into perceived compliance with Court policy.

The role of the superintendent as the central decision-maker in this instance cannot be minimized. As we view the Eastville-Westville situation, we see compliance with the Court rulings coming after the entrance of the new superintendent into the system. Occupants of other systemic positions as well as those in the larger community were virtually unchanged from the previous year, yet, in the earlier (*Engel*) instance, Court policy was disregarded, since religious practices in the schools continued. To be sure, the summer which intervened between the two school years in question saw the Court enunciate, in the *Schempp* case, a broader policy than had been articulated in the *Engel* ruling. Although the *Schempp* ruling, in its involvement with prayers and general Bible-readings in the schools, is more relevant to the Eastville-Westville situation, no one in the system was observed to have distinguished between *Engel* and *Schempp*. Thus it is clear that the activity of the two superintendents in reaction to the Court's policy was a crucial variable.

It is highly significant that action was carried out successfully by the superintendent in this community, which had merged its religious and educational life to such a considerable extent. As seen through questionnaire responses, a sizable majority in the community did not agree with the substance of the Court's policy and felt that it had exceeded its proper range of power. To most residents, in fact, the rulings expressed a disdain for the values which they held paramount; these same values had been incorporated in certain religious exercises in the school.

To understand how it happened that such exercises could be discontinued by order of the superintendent, one must consider the power resources of the superintendent himself. This individual was actively recruited from outside to bring educational expertise to this inclusive system, relating it to the larger educational world. Parents generally, in Eastville-Westville as elsewhere, acknowledge their limitations in the educational development of their children and largely forfeit their responsibility to the schools. The superintendent, then, symbolizes the professionalism of education and the extent to which the function has been delegated to actors who may not be intimately connected with the immediate social system.

The superintendent himself, as noted in Chapter 7, was acutely aware of his isolation in the community. He complained of having "no one to talk to" and found that his contacts with the local populace were almost exclusively related to his official capacity. The factors which isolated him from others in the community possibly contributed to the acceptance of his determination in this matter. He had what has been referred to earlier as "social distance." Being isolated from the demands of the more personal local environment, he was able to enunciate an impersonal policy; this would have been difficult had he been more intimately involved with the social life of the community.

While the superintendent did not personally like the extent of religious involvement in the schools under his jurisdiction, he was able to take action while presenting himself as the implementer of Supreme Court doctrine. That is, his personal motivation in this affair could be discounted as the guiding rationale for his action because a public obligation was being fulfilled. The Court as a symbol of the role of law in society became an important variable in this decision-making system, as it lowered the cost of implementing a value for the superintendent, thus increasing the probability of compliance.

Another resource which the superintendent could have used was the educational hierarchy. The superintendent's services were engaged, among other reasons, to ensure that the Eastville-Westville schools squared with the demands of the state system. Had the superintendent encountered difficulties in executing his policy, he could have appealed for a legal opinion to the State Office of Public Instruction. Had this become necessary, as we have seen, it is probable that the state office would strongly have backed the superintendent's course of action. The responsibility, then, could have been taken from the hands of the local official and transferred to the more "distant" state office. The higher office was, of course, even more removed from the peculiar exigencies of the local situation and its decision could thus be made in terms of the impersonal demands of compliance with Supreme Court determinations. Supportive action by the state office would have reinforced the superintendent in his role as "implementer" of Supreme Court policy and again would have allowed him to maintain a value at a low personal cost.

The superintendent introduced the Court's policy on religion in schools into the Eastville-Westville school district. As discussed earlier, most persons in the community would rather not have noticed what the Court said and would have proceeded with business as usual. The superintendent's action, however, related the local practices to the Court's policy. When faced with the *fait accompli,* a majority in the community—particularly among the principal elements of the educational system—generally recognized a duty to comply with this policy. Consequently, there was a broad range of support for the superintendent's action, although this support remained inarticulate and was manifested primarily in acquiescence.

It is apparent, then, that the action by the Court alone did not strike a responsive chord in the community, motivating a general compliant reaction. This was forthcoming only after the superintendent seized the initiative. The superintendent's action perhaps served to point up to many the inconsistency between local practices and Supreme Court policy; this resulted in balance restoration and a general compliant response by many in the district. Only after action by this central figure did support emerge from other important role-players. As discussed in Chapter 7, even those actors who were favorably disposed to the Court's policy refused to take the initiative—or perhaps lacked the strategic position—to bring systemic behavior into compliance.

The supportive role played by other actors in Eastville-Westville vis-à-vis the superintendent's action cannot be minimized, however. We found that there existed in the community a group of individuals who were much more highly informed concerning the Court's rulings and possibly played an important part in conveying what the Court had said. Among this group were a significantly greater proportion of individuals personally agreeing with the Court's policy than was found in the general population. Beyond this, as discussed in Chapter 8, these "influentials" were generally more affirmatively disposed toward the Court and the rules of the democratic process than were those less actively involved. These individuals did not on their own initiative attempt to have systemic behavior altered in the direction of compliance with the Court's rulings, but, after the superintendent presented the inconsistencies between local processes and national policy, they performed a valuable supportive role.

The composition of this "influential" category is of prime importance. This group was primarily composed of individuals closely associated with the educational system—the principals, teachers, and school-board members. In other words, these individuals occupied a strategic social location which seriously undercut any opposition which might have existed in the community. As emphasized earlier, the educational function is largely forfeited by parents to the formal school system, and the superintendent is brought into the system as the educational expert to relate the local school system to the larger world of education. The same considerations apply to the recruitment of other professionals—the principals and teachers in the system. An important link between the community and its school system is its board of education, but even the board members recognized their inability to cope with the plethora of technical details associated with their role. Consequently, important segments of their policy-making responsibilities devolved by default upon the "expert."

Thus, when the superintendent finds that local practices run counter to Supreme Court policy regarding religious practices in public schools, there is a general presumption of expertise on the part of the superintendent. Here is a person associated with the larger world, in contact with informed opinion, who is hired to keep the educational house in order. This responsibility presumably includes seeing to it that the local system conforms to legal expectations. The cost of opposition to the superintendent's policy regarding the lunch-time prayers in schools, then, would involve to a certain extent a denial of the superintendent's expertise. The "influentials," by supporting the superintendent's policy, reinforced his expertise power base and thus in turn reinforced the power base of the Supreme Court itself.

Parents and others in the school district may not like it, but what can be done when the school superintendent feels that the religious practices in the local schools run counter to Supreme Court policy and other principal role-players in the system support him? Clearly, little is left to those lacking such social location but to accept the superintendent's determination with acquiescence. This interpretation gains credence when one observes the pattern of response to certain related questionnaire items. A majority of respondents, for instance, agreed with the following statement (item 37): "Since local officials are responsible for what goes on in the schools, they should decide whether or not to have prayers and Bible readings, and not some far-off Court." In fact, a significantly greater proportion of the noninfluentials than influentials agreed with this statement! Also, a majority of respondents agreed with item 44: "While the Court may say that school boards may not require classroom prayers, there is no reason why teachers can't allow them on their own." As opposed to this, however, only 38 per cent of the respondents agreed with item 42: "Our school officials should do what people of the community want rather than what the

Supreme Court says that we should want." In regard to the latter two questions, there is no statistically significant difference in the response pattern between influentials and noninfluentials.

These related responses show that in Eastville-Westville it is widely recognized that the norms of the community should not be controlling in this matter. Rather, those most actively engaged in the business of education—school officials and teachers—should use their judgment. It follows, then, that, should these actors decide that local practices cannot meet the test of Court policy and must be discontinued, there is no alternative to acceptance of their decision.

Not only did important role-players in the educational system support the superintendent's action, but none of them, whatever their personal attitudes, provided a center about which opposition to the Court's policy and the superintendent's implementing action could coalesce. Perhaps the situation would have been greatly different had a key actor provided such a rallying point for the dormant opposition. For instance, the expected community outburst might have materialized had one of the ministers, a school-board member, a principal, or the former superintendent chosen to contest the superintendent's action. This did not happen. Thus, those who strongly opposed the new policy did not have strategically placed individuals who could seriously have impeded the action taken by the superintendent.

The fact must not be overlooked, however, that, while most in the community did not personally agree with the Court's policy concerning religious practices in public schools, a majority nevertheless recognized a public duty of compliance. To be sure, the characteristics of the social setting as discussed above reinforced this response. It was demonstrated in Chapter 9, however, that whether or not a duty of compliance with Court policy was acknowledged depended upon positive or negative evaluations of the Court's legitimacy and expertise, and these factors were recognized pervasively by respondents in Eastville-Westville.

It is extremely important, then, that this aura of legitimacy and expertise continue to be engendered. For lacking these resources, the influence of the Supreme Court would be diminished. Their alternatives—the elements of coercive power or of force—are very limited dimensions in this particular decision-making situation. To secure broad-scale compliance, which must largely result from activity outside the normally perceived legal sphere, the pressure must be of a more psychological nature, acting upon those who are in positions to implement the Court's policies and upon those who are affected by them.

Herein lies the importance of the dramaturgical considerations discussed in Chapter 3. There we observed the various ways in which the Court was able to create a certain "definition of the situation." Both in terms of its physical setting and in the characteristic ways the justices have historically gone about their work, the impression engendered has been one of awe, reverence, consensus, and legal certainty. While this may be of relatively minor importance in the resolution of a specific suit at bar, it is important to dramatize repeatedly to a mass audience the rule of law in the American political system.

While it is difficult to observe the impact of the dramaturgical aspects in the Eastville-Westville situation directly, its importance can be inferred. As noted so many times previously, a vast majority in this community opposed the Court's rulings in the religion-in-schools matter and felt that the Court had exceeded its proper range of power, but a recognition of the expertise and legitimacy of the Court offset the personal feelings of many. This is seen strikingly on a question which suggested specifically the idea of expertise by special training. Nearly 70 per cent of the respondents agreed with item 45: "The Constitution is a mighty complicated thing, so it's fortunate that we have a body of well-trained judges to tell us what it means." In addition to this, over a quarter of the respondents had no opinion whatsoever on item 49: "I support these decisions because they express the true meaning of constitutional church-state separation." These results dramatically indicate that for many there is a definite objectivity about the Constitution and that the work of the Supreme Court is carried on beyond the bounds of their own experience and training. Consequently, while individuals may not like the substance of Court policy on the matter, they may perceive that the justices are equipped to make the proper determinations and that they do so on strictly legal grounds. This is precisely the impression which the Court has sought to engender over the years.

In order for the Supreme Court to persist in influencing the behavior of actors in the political system who may not be under a strictly legal obligation to act, it seems imperative that the Court continue to generate the impression that its determinations result from calm deliberation and the application of esoteric rules of law. The task may become increasingly difficult, as the Court currently faces highly controversial problems of extreme importance. However, if this element is removed from the Supreme Court decision-making situation, important bases of Supreme Court power could be seriously undermined.

While the Eastville-Westville school district did comply with the Court's prayer rulings, the substance of the compliant behavior was in a form generally acceptable to the community. Certainly the schools of the district were not shorn of all vestiges of the deeply religious orientation of the community. Even though an accommodation toward religious observances was made, perhaps the core of the general rule laid down by the Court remained intact: Children were not to be forcibly exposed to the religious views of others through an officially sanctioned prayer in the lunchrooms of the elementary schools.

What happens in the lunchrooms of Eastville-Westville schools vis-à-vis Supreme Court determinations does not mean that in a larger sense there has been an *effective* decision in regard to the *Schempp* ruling. Similar action would have to be taken throughout the land. It is striking, however, that even in this relatively remote locale—one set apart from modern urban America in a number of respects—the impact of Supreme Court decision-making has been experienced. The policy enunciated by the Court has been transmitted to relevant actors in the local system through channels which are not ordinarily considered indigenous to the legal order, and action was taken in the absence of a strict and immediate legal obligation.

The point is that a Supreme Court decision in a matter of broad social concern is not fully consummated until action is taken in Eastville-Westville and innumerable other locales throughout the society. Acknowledging this, one must also recognize that a multitude of diverse roles is affected and that how the actors perform their roles has a significant bearing on the nature of the decision as it is finally and fully developed. The Supreme Court and the resources it commands are important, to be sure. The Court's formal messages may also be important symbols in the resolution of conflict at the level of implementation. Factors of perhaps supreme importance lie in the nature and characteristics of the social system which the Court's ruling penetrates. The ultimate disposition of the issue may depend primarily upon the resources that the relevant actors at this level bring to bear—resources which originate in the immediate social milieu. For these reasons the compliance process may be studied as profitably in Eastville-Westville as anywhere to see the interplay of social and psychological factors which are necessarily involved.

APPENDIX A

Methodological Considerations

THE COURT'S HANDLING of the religious issue was selected primarily because it presents the Supreme Court decision-making system at its broadest point. That is, this issue allows one to observe the activity of a number of actors who are not normal participants in the legal system. Also of importance was the fact that the issue had some relevance in this locale because Champaign, also in Illinois, was the site of the *McCollum* case of 1948, involving religious instruction on school premises during school time. The initial intention was to conduct this study in the cities of Champaign and Urbana. It was soon discovered that the issue there was dead and that the recent *Engel* and *Schempp* rulings thus had no relevance.

Finding a suitable locale in Illinois—a necessity for the author, who had teaching commitments in Urbana—was no mean task. Illinois school systems do not in most cases have religious devotional exercises in their classrooms, as Illinois law generally discourages such practices. Thus, as in Champaign-Urbana, the recent rulings have little relevance in most places throughout the state. Fortunately, the Eastville-Westville district was called to the author's attention by a fellow graduate student who resided there.

This early personal contact in the community and its educational system was extremely helpful in acquainting the author with conditions there, as well as providing a chance for sizing up various actors in the community before the field work commenced. Of most importance was the author's access to the superintendent, who was a most willing respondent on innumerable occasions and was tremendously helpful in all phases of the study. This was most fortuitous, for the superintendent was the central actor in the compliance situation in Eastville-Westville.

• *The Interviews and the Questionnaire*

Starting with the superintendent, interviews were conducted to determine the way in which the issue impinged upon the local system. Following the superintendent, the principals, the former superintendent, and all the school-board members were interviewed. Along with questions attempting to ascertain their feelings about the issue, the channels through which they had been apprised of it, and the expectations they perceived others in the system to hold in this regard, the interviewees were asked to name the individuals who took a more active part than others in the affairs of the community—in other words, the "influentials."

Those who were named most often were then interviewed. It became clear that most of these persons took very little part in the resolution of this issue in the community, although most had very definite views on the subject. The issue was primarily resolved in the educational system, with little interference from those without.

Three hundred questionnaires were then sent through the mail. One parent of each school child received a questionnaire, as well as all the teachers and those who had previously been interviewed. Great pains were taken to obtain a large return. An article describing the study was run in the local papers. Three days later a letter, outlining the study and asking for cooperation, was sent to those who were to receive the questionnaires. A copy of the newspaper clipping was enclosed. After another three-day period, the questionnaire was mailed with a covering letter and a self-addressed stamped envelope for a first-class-mail return. Copies of the newspaper article and the letters appear at the end of this Appendix.

In all, 176 questionnaires were returned, a response rate of nearly 59 per cent. The following is the distribution over time of the returned questionnaires:

1st week	71	After phone call	18
2nd week	22	After second letter	4
3rd week	10	After second phone call	20
4th week (after letter)	20	Other	6
5th week	5		

As one expects in mail surveys, the bulk of the responses came within the first three weeks. After the third week a follow-up letter was sent to half of the nonrespondents, while the other half received another questionnaire and another stamped envelope. Half of those receiving additional questionnaires had a code number plainly marked on the questionnaire, while the code number was concealed on those going to the other half. Those who received a second copy of the questionnaire did not respond to any greater degree than those who got only the letters. Nor did concealing the code number seem to make any difference. In fact, some who received an apparently uncoded questionnaire even returned their original questionnaires, which were quite obviously coded. All who were interviewed returned their questionnaires with the exception of the Eastville Methodist minister and the elderly teacher of the adult Sunday-school class of that church.

After the fifth week, telephone calls were made to the nonrespondents, and letters were sent to those who had no phone. Two weeks later, follow-up calls were made. As the above summary indicates, phone calls were the most effective of the follow-up devices. On the first calls little antagonism was expressed, as most excused themselves for "just not getting around to filling it out." More resistance was encountered on the second calls. By this point it became clear that few more returns could be expected. There were no systematic variations in responses related to point in time at which the questionnaire was returned.

The recognized difficulty with the mail questionnaires is the problem of generalization of the findings. One is able to generalize only to the sample of those actually returning the questionnaire, for it is difficult to establish whether or not the respondents systematically differ from the nonrespondents. If there is a systematic difference between the two groups, one cannot validly generalize to the population receiving the questionnaire. Some insight into the nature of at least some of the nonrespondents was received, however. At the time of the second phone call, the author reviewed the list of nonrespondents with the superintendent's secretary, a local woman who knew most of the people in the district. She identified a number of the nonrespondents as not having the capacity to complete a questionnaire such as this. It is admitted that the questionnaire, which is contained in Appendix B, is rather difficult and probably remote for many in Eastville-Westville. Under these conditions, a response rate of 60 per cent is considered fairly high—higher than anticipated by the superintendent on the basis of his experience in distributing informational forms to the parents in the district. Nevertheless, the problem of generalizing the findings remains.

Copies of the newspaper clipping and the letters follow.

SCHOOL DISTRICT IS SITE OF STUDY

The School District has been selected as a site for an important study. Richard M. Johnson, a University of Illinois political scientist, is investigating how the public is reacting to recent United States Supreme Court decisions involving religious practices in the public schools. This district has been chosen as being representative of rural school districts in general.

During the past two months, Mr. Johnson has been interviewing school officials and board members as well as certain other people in the two communities and the surrounding areas. Also, however, he is interested in finding out what other members of the community think about this issue. So, in the near future parents of school children in the district will be receiving by mail a questionnaire designed to discover their opinions.

Mr. Johnson hopes that all those who receive the questionnaire will find it convenient to fill it out and return it to him. It is necessary, he states, to get as large a return as possible in order to make this a meaningful study. He says if the people of the district will respond to the questionnaire with as much enthusiasm and cooperation as those who have already been interviewed, this is bound to be a successful project.

First Letter

Department of Political Science
University of Illinois
May 11, 1964

Dear Parent:

Perhaps you remember seeing the enclosed clipping in last Friday's (*Eastville*) *Tribune* or (*Westville*) *Record.* As you have read, the Eastville–Westville School District has been chosen as a site for a most important study. This is an appeal to you personally for your cooperation.

In the past few years, the United States Supreme Court has handed down some decisions regarding religious practices in public schools which have stirred up a great deal of controversy. Currently, for instance, the U.S. Congress is considering a number of proposals which could change by constitutional amendment what the Court has said.

As a political scientist, I am interested in finding out what people in a community such as yours think about religious practices in the schools and the Court's handling of the issue. I have already talked with many of your school officials about this, but now I would like to know your feelings as well.

In the next few days you will receive by mail a questionnaire which I hope you will complete and return to me as quickly as convenient. Rest assured that the answers you give are of scholarly interest only and will be kept *strictly confidential.* A stamped, self-addressed envelope will be enclosed with the questionnaire for your convenience. May I again say that the success of this study depends upon the return of the questionnaire.

The cooperation received so far from people in your community has been wonderful. If you respond with the same enthusiasm and cooperation, we certainly will have worked together for an important and meaningful study.

Sincerely yours,
RICHARD M. JOHNSON

Letter Accompanying Questionnaire

Department of Political Science
University of Illinois
May 15, 1964

Dear Parents:

I assume that you received my letter of May 11. There I asked for your personal cooperation in a study of your community's reaction to recent United States Supreme Court decisions regarding religious practices in public schools.

Enclosed you will find the questionnaire which I hope you will promptly fill out and return to me in the stamped, self-addressed envelope. May I remind you that your answers are of scholarly interest only and will be kept *strictly confidential.*

Since the success of this study depends upon you completing and returning the questionnaire, I naturally hope that it will be convenient for you to do so. Actually, you will probably find it interesting and not at all time-consuming to answer this list of questions.

Thank you in advance for your splendid cooperation.

Sincerely yours,
RICHARD M. JOHNSON

Letter to Teachers

Department of Political Science
University of Illinois
May 13, 1964

Dear Teacher:

Perhaps you remember seeing the enclosed clipping in last Friday's (*Eastville*) *Tribune* or (*Westville*) *Record.* As you have read, the Eastville-Westville School District has been chosen as a site for a most important study. This is an appeal to you personally for your cooperation.

In the past few years, the United States Supreme Court has handed down some decisions regarding religious practices in public schools which have stirred up a great deal of controversy. Currently, for instance, the U.S. Congress is considering a number of proposals which could change by constitutional amendment what the Court has said.

As a political scientist, I am interested in finding out what people in a community such as yours think about religious practices in the schools and the Court's handling of the issue. Your superintendent, principal, and school-board members have given me their views in interviews earlier this spring. Now I am particularly interested in finding out how you as a teacher feel about this matter.

Consequently, I hope you will complete this questionnaire and promptly return it to me in the stamped, self-addressed envelope which is enclosed. Rest assured that the answers you give are of scholarly interest only and will be kept *strictly confidential.* Parents of the school children in the district are also receiving this questionnaire by mail this week.

The success of this study, of course, depends upon the return of the questionnaire. I hope that you will find the answering of these questions interesting and thought-provoking. Thank you in advance for your cooperation.

Sincerely yours,
RICHARD M. JOHNSON

First Follow-Up Letter

Department of Political Science
University of Illinois
June 4, 1964

Dear Parent:

A few weeks ago you, as well as all the other parents of the (Eastville-Westville) School District, were invited to participate in an important study of public reaction to the U.S. Supreme Court decisions regarding religious practices in public schools. As you may remember, you were asked to kindly complete a questionnaire and return it to me.

The response to the questionnaire has been quite gratifying, as many of your neighbors have already returned it in the stamped, self-addressed envelope provided. In fact, a number of people have written and said how much they enjoyed the opportunity to participate in this worthwhile project. For instance, one person added a note, saying: "I am very much interested in what you are doing, and I might add that your questions are extremely thought-provoking."

I know that this is a very busy time of year for you, so if you haven't had the opportunity to complete the questionnaire as yet, I do hope that you find it convenient to do so in the near future. Since you may have misplaced the questionnaire, I am enclosing another copy as well as another stamped, self-addressed envelope for your convenience. If you have already completed this task, please disregard this letter; and I thank you very much for your co-operation.

Sincerely yours,
RICHARD M. JOHNSON

Final Follow-Up Letter

Department of Political Science
University of Illinois
June 23, 1964

Dear Parent:

This is the final appeal for your participation in my study. A good many of your friends and neighbors have filled out the questionnaire and returned it to me in the stamped envelope which I provided. Since the value of this study depends upon a large return of the questionnaire, I hope that, if you have not already done so, you will complete the task promptly. If you wish your opinions to be included, you must act in the next week, for the time has come for me to sit down and analyze what people have been telling me the past few months.

I sincerely hope that you choose to help me in this timely and important study. Thank you again for your cooperation.

Sincerely yours,
RICHARD M. JOHNSON

APPENDIX B

Questionnaire and Response Frequencies

FOLLOWING IS THE QUESTIONNAIRE administered to some three hundred individuals in Eastville-Westville, as described in Appendix A. Response frequencies for each question are included in this summary, with the respective percentages appearing within parentheses.

Please *check* the most appropriate answers to the following questions:

1. Approximately how long have you lived in this community?

1. Less than 1 year	12 (6.8)	5. 12 to 20 years	23 (13.1)
2. 1 to 3 years	10 (5.7)	6. Over 20 years	86 (48.9)
3. 3 to 6 years	19 (10.8)	Other	5 (2.8)
4. 6 to 12 years	20 (11.4)	Blank	1 (0.6)

2. Have you lived here all your life?

Yes 60 (34.1) No 115 (65.3) Blank 1 (0.6)

3. What is your present occupation?

1. Farmer	64 (36.4)	6. Housewife	31 (17.6)
2. Businessman	14 (8.0)	7. Workman	25 (14.2)
3. Clerical or sales	4 (2.3)	8. Other occupation (Specify below)	
4. Teacher	27 (15.3)	________________	6 (3.4)
5. Professional	4 (2.3)	Blank	1 (0.6)

4. As for religion, which of the following do you consider yourself?

1. Methodist	97 (55.1)	6. Catholic	6 (3.4)
2. Jewish	0	7. No religion	4 (2.3)
3. Baptist	17 (9.7)	8. Other (Specify below)	
4. Lutheran	6 (3.4)	________________	11 (6.3)
5. Christian	34 (19.3)	Blank	1 (0.6)

5. Are you a member of a church?

Yes	150 (85.2)	No	26 (14.8)

6. About how often, if ever, have you attended religious services in the past year?

1. Once a week or more	98 (55.7)	4. A few times	36 (20.5)
2. 2 or 3 times a month	24 (13.6)	5. Never	9 (5.1)
3. Once a month	6 (3.4)	Blank	3 (1.7)

7. To what extent do you feel you participate in church activities in addition to attending services? (e.g., teaching Sunday School, belonging to organizations, being an officer, etc.)

1. Very much	43 (24.4)	4. None at all	27 (15.3)
2. Average amount	71 (40.3)	5. Not applicable	3 (1.7)
3. Not much	31 (17.6)	Blank	1 (0.6)

8. Do you consider your religious activities more or less important to you than your other activities?

1. More important	91 (51.7)	4. Not applicable	10 (5.7)
2. About the same	53 (30.1)	Blank	2 (1.1)
3. Less important	20 (11.4)		

9. Since World War II the Supreme Court has handled a number of cases involving religion in public schools. How familiar are you with what the Court has said about some of these matters?

1. Very familiar	7 (4.0)	4. Not familiar at all	9 (5.1)
2. Generally familiar	93 (52.8)	Blank	1 (0.6)
3. Not very familiar	66 (37.5)		

10. Do you feel that the following statements are accurate summaries of what the Court has said about some of these matters?

    1. A state legislature may not prescribe an official prayer to be said in public school classrooms by students.

a. Yes, accurate	122 (69.3)	c. Don't know	13 (7.4)
b. No, inaccurate	36 (20.5)	Blank	5 (2.8)

    2. A school board may not require that the Lord's Prayer be used in devotional services in public school classrooms.

a. Yes, accurate	114 (64.8)	c. Don't know	19 (10.8)
b. No, inaccurate	38 (21.6)	Blank	5 (2.8)

    3. Public school officials may not release students for instruction by church representatives outside the schools.

a. Yes, accurate	42 (23.9)	c. Don't know	68 (38.6)
b. No, inaccurate	61 (34.7)	Blank	5 (2.8)

4. Religiously garbed nuns may not teach in public schools.

a. Yes, accurate	31 (17.6)	c. Don't know	69 (39.2)
b. No, inaccurate	70 (39.8)	Blank	6 (3.4)

11. So far as you understand the Court's decisions in this area, do you feel that religious programs such as baccalaureate services in the schools are illegal?

1. Yes	16 (9.1)	3. Don't know	16 (9.1)
2. No	141 (80.1)	Blank	3 (1.7)

12. If you remember, please indicate how you *first* became aware of *any* of the Court decisions concerning religion in schools.

1. Newspapers	48 (27.3)	7. I don't remember	14 (8.0)
2. Magazines	0	8. Other means (Specify below)	
3. Radio or TV	30 (17.1)	______________	0
4. Church literature	1 (0.57)	Combination of above	80 (45.5)
5. Minister's sermons	0	Blank	2 (1.1)
6. Personal discussions	1 (0.57)		

13. Which of the above sources (question 12) do you feel was *most helpful* to you when forming an opinion about the Court's handling of this issue? (Please check the appropriate number.)

1. 45 (25.6)	5. 6 (3.4)
2. 9 (5.1)	6. 18 (10.2)
3. 30 (17.1)	7. 6 (3.4)
4. 5 (2.8)	8. 39 (22.2)
	Blank 18 (10.2)

14. Do you feel that you know more about the Court's decisions about religious practices in schools than its decisions in other areas, such as school desegregation or legislative districting?

1. Know more about religion decisions	38 (21.6)
2. Equally informed about religion and other decisions	75 (42.6)
3. Know less about religion decisions	32 (18.2)
4. Not informed about the work of the Court at all	20 (11.4)
Blank	11 (6.3)

15. Do you recall discussing with others the Court's decisions involving religious practices in schools?

Yes 144 (81.8) No 24 (13.6) Blank 8 (4.6)

16. With whom do you recall discussing these decisions the most?

1. My family	26 (14.8)	4. Schoolteachers	6 (3.4)
2. Fellow workers	10 (5.7)	5. No one	13 (7.4)
3. Neighbors	12 (6.8)	6. My clergyman	1 (0.6)

7. Church members	10 (5.7)	________________	0
8. I don't recall	6 (3.4)	Combination of above	85 (48.3)
9. With others (Specify below)		Blank	7 (4.0)

17. Do you recall ever informing others of any of these decisions who had not previously heard of them?

Yes 35 (19.9) No 135 (76.7) Blank 6 (3.4)

18. If yes, whom do you recall informing about the decisions? (Please check the appropriate number below from question 16 items.)

1. 10 (5.7)	7. 2 (1.1)		
2. 3 (1.7)	8. 0		
3. 7 (4.0)	9. 0		
4. 5 (2.8)		Combination of above	17 (9.7)
5. 7 (4.0)		Blank	125 (71.0)
6. 0			

19. Compared with other people you know, are you more or less likely to be asked for information or advice about these matters?

1. More likely	36 (20.5)	3. Don't know	66 (37.5)
2. Less likely	70 (39.8)	Blank	4 (2.3)

20. Do you recall ever asking someone to explain any of these decisions to you?

Yes 56 (31.8) No 115 (65.3) Blank 5 (2.8)

21. If yes, whom did you ask to explain these decisions to you? (Again, please check the appropriate question 16 item.)

1. 11 (6.3)	7. 3 (1.7)		
2. 5 (2.8)	8. 0		
3. 7 (4.0)	9. 0		
4. 6 (3.4)		Combination of above	16 (9.1)
5. 5 (2.8)		Blank	119 (67.6)
6. 4 (2.3)			

22. Are any practices of a religious nature currently going on in your local schools?

Yes	79 (44.9)	Don't know	39 (22.2)
No	52 (29.6)	Blank	6 (3.4)

23. If religious practices are going on, what is their nature? (Open-ended)

1. None or blank	96 (54.5)	5. Morning prayers	2 (1.1)
2. Silent prayer	21 (11.9)	6. Religious programs	13 (7.4)
3. Blessing of food	28 (15.9)	7. Combination of above	10 (5.7)
4. W.C.T.U. programs	6 (3.4)		

24. How would you describe your feelings about the way your school officials have handled the question of religion in school?

1. Strongly approve	15 (8.5)	5. Strongly disapprove	11 (6.3)
2. Generally approve	71 (40.3)	6. Not familiar	33 (18.8)
3. No opinion	26 (14.8)	Blank	3 (1.7)
4. Generally disapprove	17 (9.7)		

25. Do you recall ever telling any school official of your feelings about religious practices in the schools?

Yes 44 (25.0) No 127 (72.2) Blank 5 (2.8)

26. If the Supreme Court would declare unconstitutional Christmas programs in public schools, what do you feel your local school officials should do about such programs in your schools?

1. Order a stop to such programs	22 (12.5)
2. Take no action; allow these programs to continue	44 (25.0)
3. Order our Christmas programs to continue	33 (18.8)
4. Draw up a substitute arrangement to satisfy both religious as well as legal needs	60 (34.1)
5. Other action (Please specify) ______________	10 (5.7)
Blank	7 (4.0)

27. Do you agree or disagree with what the Court has said about religious practices in public schools?

1. Strongly agree	9 (5.1)	5. Strongly disagree	23 (13.1)
2. Agree	36 (20.5)	6. Not familiar	15 (8.5)
3. No opinion	20 (11.4)	Blank	4 (2.3)
4. Disagree	69 (39.2)		

28. Some people say that Supreme Court judges decide many questions on the basis of which political party they belong to. Do you agree or disagree with this?

1. Strongly agree	9 (5.1)	4. Disagree	63 (35.8)
2. Agree	25 (14.2)	5. Strongly disagree	15 (8.5)
3. No opinion	59 (33.5)	Blank	5 (2.8)

29. Do you think that the Supreme Court has been too liberal or too conservative in its decisions in recent years?

1. Too conservative	20 (11.4)	4. No opinion	67 (38.1)
2. About right	47 (26.7)	Blank	8 (4.6)
3. Too liberal	34 (19.3)		

30. Has your opinion of the Supreme Court gone up or down since World War II?

1. Has gone down	54 (30.7)	2. No change	42 (23.9)

3. Has gone up	17 (9.7)	Blank	3 (1.7)
4. No opinion	60 (34.1)		

31. Some charge that the Supreme Court judges give preference to certain special interests such as labor unions or big business. Do you agree or disagree?

1. Strongly agree	4 (2.3)	4. Disagree	43 (24.4)
2. Agree	45 (25.6)	5. Strongly disagree	5 (2.8)
3. No opinion	77 (43.8)	Blank	2 (1.1)

32. There are those who say that some of the Court judges are pro-Communist. How do you feel about this?

1. Strongly agree	3 (1.7)	4. Disagree	50 (28.4)
2. Agree	12 (6.8)	5. Strongly disagree	15 (8.5)
3. No opinion	92 (52.3)	Blank	4 (2.3)

33. Some people think that the Supreme Court helps the city folk more than the small town or farm people. How do you feel?

1. Strongly agree	7 (4.0)	4. Disagree	49 (27.8)
2. Agree	30 (17.1)	5. Strongly disagree	9 (5.1)
3. No opinion	80 (45.5)	Blank	1 (0.6)

While many people agree with what the Supreme Court has said about religion in schools, many others have criticized the Court. We would like to know what you think about various aspects of this problem. Please mark each of the following statements on the line at the right as to how much you agree or disagree with it. *Please mark each statement* with one of the following symbols:

+ 1: I agree a little	− 1: I disagree a little
+ 2: I agree pretty much	− 2: I disagree pretty much
+ 3: I agree very much	− 3: I disagree very much

0: I have no opinion

Example: Apple pie is the best kind of pie. + 3

34. No matter what one may think about religious practices, if the Supreme Court says they are unconstitutional, one has the duty to accept the decision and act accordingly.

+ 3 41 (23.3)	0 5 (2.8)	− 1 25 (14.2)
+ 2 26 (14.8)		− 2 17 (9.7)
+ 1 21 (11.9)	Blank 11 (6.3)	− 3 30 (17.1)

35. Although the Court should interpret the Constitution, it has gone too far when it starts telling us that we can't pray in our schools.

+ 3 75 (42.6)	0 4 (2.3)	− 1 7 (4.0)
+ 2 32 (18.2)		− 2 11 (6.3)
+ 1 18 (10.2)	Blank 13 (7.4)	− 3 16 (9.1)

36. Even though we may want to continue our local practices, we can't fight the power of the federal courts.

+ 3 26 (14.8)	0 11 (6.3)	− 1 19 (10.8)
+ 2 16 (9.1)		− 2 22 (12.5)
+ 1 18 (10.2)	Blank 13 (7.4)	− 3 51 (29.0)

37. Since local officials are responsible for what goes on in the schools, they should decide whether or not to have prayers and Bible readings and not some far-off court.

+ 3 49 (27.8)	0 7 (4.0)	− 1 17 (9.7)
+ 2 26 (14.8)		− 2 17 (9.7)
+ 1 16 (9.1)	Blank 16 (9.1)	− 3 28 (15.9)

38. Supreme Court judges have the natural abilities to tell us what the Constitution really means.

+ 3 22 (12.5)	0 17 (9.7)	− 1 19 (10.8)
+ 2 32 (18.2)		− 2 18 (10.2)
+ 1 22 (12.5)	Blank 17 (9.7)	− 3 29 (16.5)

39. While I might think that religious practices in schoolrooms are good, in the long run the idea of "separation of church and state" is beneficial to religion.

+ 3 55 (31.3)	0 18 (10.2)	− 1 12 (6.8)
+ 2 25 (14.2)		− 2 14 (8.0)
+ 1 18 (10.2)	Blank 15 (8.5)	− 3 19 (10.8)

40. The problem with these decisions is that they aid undesirable Godless groups.

+ 3 58 (33.0)	0 23 (13.1)	− 1 6 (3.4)
+ 2 27 (15.3)		− 2 10 (5.7)
+ 1 18 (10.2)	Blank 16 (9.1)	− 3 18 (10.2)

41. No matter what local school officials think, they must do what the Court says to prevent the federal government from moving in and using force.

+ 3 27 (15.3)	0 22 (12.5)	− 1 15 (8.5)
+ 2 35 (19.9)		− 2 8 (4.6)
+ 1 21 (11.9)	Blank 18 (10.2)	− 3 30 (17.1)

42. Our school officials should do what the people of the community want rather than what the Supreme Court says that we should want.

+ 3 33 (18.8)	0 7 (4.0)	− 1 24 (13.6)
+ 2 15 (8.5)		− 2 35 (19.9)
+ 1 19 (10.8)	Blank 17 (9.7)	− 3 26 (14.8)

43. The positive good for the child connected with religion in the schools more than offsets knowing that you are not doing exactly as the Supreme Court has said.

+ 3 30 (17.1)	0 23 (13.1)	− 1 18 (10.2)
+ 2 26 (14.8)		− 2 20 (11.4)
+ 1 15 (8.5)	Blank 18 (10.2)	− 3 26 (14.8)

44. While the Court may say that school boards may not require classroom prayers, there is no reason why teachers can't allow them on their own.

+ 3 48 (27.3)	0 16 (9.1)	− 1 12 (6.8)
+ 2 24 (13.6)		− 2 14 (8.0)
+ 1 18 (10.2)	Blank 18 (10.2)	− 3 26 (14.8)

45. The Constitution is a mighty complicated thing, so it's fortunate that we have a body of well-trained judges to tell us what it means.

+ 3 49 (27.8)	0 17 (9.7)	− 1 8 (4.6)
+ 2 53 (30.1)		− 2 3 (1.7)
+ 1 21 (11.9)	Blank 15 (8.5)	− 3 10 (5.7)

46. The real problem lies in this: these decisions are one more step toward making the U.S. a Godless state.

+ 3 40 (22.7)	0 13 (7.4)	− 1 11 (6.3)
+ 2 20 (11.4)		− 2 16 (9.1)
+ 1 25 (14.2)	Blank 16 (9.1)	− 3 35 (19.9)

47. Although we may disagree, we must accept what the Court has said, since it has traditionally had the job of telling us what the Constitution means.

+ 3 29 (16.5)	0 14 (8.0)	− 1 19 (10.8)
+ 2 36 (20.5)		− 2 17 (9.7)
+ 1 22 (12.5)	Blank 16 (9.1)	− 3 23 (13.1)

48. These decisions may seem harmless, but they fit into the general trend in this country toward Godlessness, corruption, crime, divorce, and delinquency.

+ 3 53 (30.1)	0 12 (6.8)	− 1 6 (3.4)
+ 2 22 (12.5)		− 2 12 (6.8)
+ 1 19 (10.8)	Blank 14 (8.0)	− 3 38 (21.6)

49. I support these decisions because they express the true meaning of constitutional church-state separation.

+ 3 18 (10.2)	0 29 (16.5)	− 1 18 (10.2)
+ 2 22 (12.5)		− 2 17 (9.7)
+ 1 20 (11.4)	Blank 19 (10.8)	− 3 33 (18.8)

50. While one may dislike what the Court says at times, one must accept its decisions to be a good citizen.

+ 3 30 (17.1)	0 4 (2.3)	− 1 23 (13.1)
+ 2 48 (27.3)		− 2 13 (7.4)
+ 1 23 (13.1)	Blank 14 (8.0)	− 3 21 (11.9)

The best answer to each of the more general statements below is *your personal opinion.* We have tried to cover many points of view. Whether you agree or disagree with any statement, you can be sure that many other people feel the same way you do. Again mark *each* statement at the right as to how much you agree or disagree with it according to the same following key:

+ 1: I agree a little	– 1: I disagree a little
+ 2: I agree pretty much	– 2: I disagree pretty much
+ 3: I agree very much	– 3: I disagree very much

0: I have no opinion

51. When private enterprise does not do the job, it is up to the government to step in and meet the public's need for housing, water power, and the like.

+ 3 32 (18.2)	0 8 (4.6)	– 1 9 (5.1)
+ 2 39 (22.2)		– 2 16 (9.1)
+ 1 39 (22.2)	Blank 14 (8.0)	– 3 19 (10.8)

52. Most people today can be trusted.

+ 3 31 (17.6)	0 2 (1.1)	– 1 18 (10.2)
+ 2 58 (33.0)		– 2 20 (11.4)
+ 1 24 (13.6)	Blank 10 (5.7)	– 3 13 (7.4)

53. Despite all the newspaper and TV coverage, national and international happenings rarely seem as interesting as events that occur in the local community.

+ 3 19 (10.8)	0 3 (1.7)	– 1 19 (10.8)
+ 2 33 (18.8)		– 2 40 (22.7)
+ 1 15 (8.5)	Blank 11 (6.3)	– 3 36 (20.5)

54. In times like these, a person must be pretty selfish if he considers primarily his own happiness.

+ 3 63 (35.8)	0 4 (2.3)	– 1 10 (5.7)
+ 2 53 (30.1)		– 2 11 (6.3)
+ 1 13 (7.4)	Blank 12 (6.8)	– 3 10 (5.7)

55. Everyone should believe in and practice some religion.

+ 3 122 (69.3)	0 4 (2.3)	– 1 3 (1.7)
+ 2 18 (10.2)		– 2 4 (2.3)
+ 1 9 (5.1)	Blank 10 (5.7)	– 3 6 (3.4)

56. Men like Henry Ford or J. P. Morgan, who overcame all competition on the road to success, are models for all young people to admire and imitate.

+ 3 30 (17.1)	0 16 (9.1)	– 1 25 (14.2)
+ 2 21 (11.9)		– 2 22 (12.5)
+ 1 24 (13.6)	Blank 13 (7.4)	– 3 25 (14.2)

57. When it comes to differences of opinion in religion, we must be careful not to compromise with those who believe differently from the way we do.

+ 3 33 (18.8)	0 5 (2.8)	− 1 23 (13.1)
+ 2 19 (10.8)		− 2 42 (23.9)
+ 1 10 (5.7)	Blank 12 (6.8)	− 3 32 (18.2)

58. The government should own and operate all public utilities (railroads, gas, electricity, etc.)

+ 3 5 (2.8)	0 9 (5.1)	− 1 4 (2.3)
+ 2 1 (0.6)		− 2 22 (12.5)
+ 1 3 (1.7)	Blank 11 (6.3)	− 3 121 (68.8)

59. Most people are more inclined to look out for themselves than to help others.

+ 3 44 (25.0)	0 1 (0.6)	− 1 11 (6.3)
+ 2 55 (31.3)		− 2 18 (10.2)
+ 1 30 (17.1)	Blank 9 (5.1)	− 3 8 (4.6)

60. All children should attend Sunday School or have some other opportunity to learn about their religious heritage.

+ 3 132 (75.0)	0 1 (0.6)	− 1 3 (1.7)
+ 2 22 (12.5)		− 2 2 (1.1)
+ 1 4 (2.3)	Blank 9 (5.1)	− 3 3 (1.7)

61. Generally, full economic security is bad; most men wouldn't work if they didn't need the money for eating and living.

+ 3 40 (22.7)	0 3 (1.7)	− 1 18 (10.2)
+ 2 22 (12.5)		− 2 32 (18.2)
+ 1 29 (16.5)	Blank 10 (5.7)	− 3 22 (12.5)

62. In the history of mankind, there has probably been just a handful of really great men.

+ 3 22 (12.5)	0 8 (4.6)	− 1 23 (13.1)
+ 2 21 (11.9)		− 2 37 (21.0)
+ 1 7 (4.0)	Blank 9 (5.1)	− 3 49 (27.8)

63. Strong labor unions are necessary if the working man is to get greater security and a better standard of living.

+ 3 21 (11.9)	0 14 (8.0)	− 1 28 (15.9)
+ 2 36 (20.5)		− 2 18 (10.2)
+ 1 25 (14.2)	Blank 9 (5.1)	− 3 25 (14.2)

64. If you don't watch out for yourself, people will take advantage of you.

+ 3 30 (17.1)	0 0	− 1 17 (9.7)

+ 2 42 (23.9)		− 2 14 (8.0)
+ 1 53 (30.1)	Blank 11 (6.3)	− 3 9 (5.1)

65. A man who does not believe in some great cause has not really lived.

+ 3 54 (30.7)	0 10 (5.7)	− 1 17 (9.7)
+ 2 42 (23.9)		− 2 10 (5.7)
+ 1 22 (12.5)	Blank 14 (8.0)	− 3 7 (4.0)

66. I have greater respect for the man who is well established in his local community than one who is widely known in his field but has no local roots.

+ 3 35 (19.8)	0 13 (7.4)	− 1 24 (13.7)
+ 2 25 (14.2)		− 2 35 (19.8)
+ 1 13 (7.4)	Blank 15 (8.5)	− 3 16 (9.1)

67. The only way to do away with poverty is to make basic changes in our political and economic system.

+ 3 17 (9.7)	0 18 (10.2)	− 1 18 (10.2)
+ 2 18 (10.2)		− 2 29 (16.5)
+ 1 25 (14.2)	Blank 19 (10.8)	− 3 32 (18.2)

68. The best way to foster the moral development of civilization is through organized religion.

+ 3 35 (19.8)	0 8 (4.6)	− 1 18 (10.2)
+ 2 28 (15.9)		− 2 23 (13.1)
+ 1 22 (12.5)	Blank 15 (8.5)	− 3 27 (15.4)

69. There are a number of people I have come to hate because of the things they stand for.

+ 3 4 (2.3)	0 7 (4.0)	− 1 18 (10.2)
+ 2 3 (1.7)		− 2 34 (19.3)
+ 1 14 (8.0)	Blank 18 (10.2)	− 3 78 (44.3)

70. No one should be allowed to earn more than $60,000 a year.

+ 3 8 (4.6)	0 12 (6.8)	− 1 14 (8.0)
+ 2 7 (4.0)		− 2 25 (14.2)
+ 1 8 (4.6)	Blank 14 (8.0)	− 3 88 (50.0)

71. The most rewarding organizations a person can belong to are local ones rather than large national organizations.

+ 3 17 (9.7)	0 11 (6.3)	− 1 21 (11.9)
+ 2 40 (22.7)		− 2 29 (16.5)
+ 1 22 (12.5)	Blank 16 (9.1)	− 3 20 (11.4)

72. When it comes right down to it, no one is going to care much what happens to you.

+ 3 5 (2.8)	0 0	− 1 31 (17.6)
+ 2 13 (7.4)		− 2 49 (27.8)
+ 1 10 (5.7)	Blank 14 (8.0)	− 3 54 (30.7)

73. The government should develop a program of health insurance and medical care.

+ 3 24 (13.6)	0 9 (5.1)	− 1 12 (6.8)
+ 2 30 (17.1)		− 2 15 (8.5)
+ 1 19 (10.8)	Blank 16 (9.1)	− 3 51 (29.0)

74. Human nature is fundamentally cooperative.

+ 3 41 (23.3)	0 5 (2.8)	− 1 5 (2.8)
+ 2 60 (34.1)		− 2 7 (4.0)
+ 1 34 (19.2)	Blank 17 (9.7)	− 3 7 (4.0)

75. A person who gets enthusiastic about too many causes is bound to be a pretty wishy-washy sort of person.

+ 3 26 (14.8)	0 8 (4.6)	− 1 21 (11.9)
+ 2 33 (18.7)		− 2 29 (16.5)
+ 1 33 (18.7)	Blank 12 (6.8)	− 3 14 (8.0)

76. To compromise with our political opponents is dangerous because it leads to the betrayal of our own side.

+ 3 10 (5.7)	0 10 (5.7)	− 1 36 (20.4)
+ 2 16 (9.1)		− 2 57 (32.4)
+ 1 8 (4.6)	Blank 16 (9.1)	− 3 23 (13.1)

77. Under no conditions should a woman have sexual relations until she is married.

+ 3 107 (60.8)	0 5 (2.8)	− 1 15 (8.5)
+ 2 18 (10.2)		− 2 4 (2.3)
+ 1 8 (4.6)	Blank 16 (9.1)	− 3 3 (1.7)

78. At this time, powerful "big business" is a greater danger than powerful "big unions" to our national welfare.

+ 3 16 (9.1)	0 32 (18.1)	− 1 29 (16.5)
+ 2 12 (6.8)		− 2 29 (16.5)
+ 1 15 (8.5)	Blank 19 (10.8)	− 3 24 (13.6)

79. I feel I get better information and advice about things from out-of-town connections than from anyone locally.

+ 3 16 (9.1)	0 7 (4.0)	− 1 35 (19.9)
+ 2 28 (15.9)		− 2 30 (17.0)
+ 1 19 (10.8)	Blank 17 (9.7)	− 3 24 (13.6)

80. We need more government controls over business practices and profits.

+ 3 8 (4.6)	0 6 (3.4)	− 1 30 (17.0)
+ 2 12 (6.8)		− 2 29 (16.5)
+ 1 18 (10.2)	Blank 12 (6.8)	− 3 61 (34.7)

81. Of all the different philosophies which exist in the world there is probably only one which is correct.

+ 3 23 (13.1)	0 9 (5.1)	− 1 25 (14.2)
+ 2 10 (5.7)		− 2 36 (20.5)
+ 1 9 (5.1)	Blank 17 (9.7)	− 3 47 (26.7)

82. Labor unions in large corporations should be given a larger part in deciding company policy.

+ 3 10 (5.7)	0 19 (10.8)	− 1 23 (13.1)
+ 2 10 (5.7)		− 2 36 (20.5)
+ 1 18 (10.2)	Blank 18 (10.2)	− 3 42 (23.9)

THANK YOU AGAIN FOR YOUR FINE COOPERATION

INDEX

Index